LOVE & SEX

in

D. H. Lawrence

LOVE & SEX
in
D. H. Lawrence

DAVID ELLIS

CLEMSON UNIVERSITY PRESS

For John Worthen

People have made of the pleasure associated with sexual intercourse something *sacred*, just like epilepsy with which it has more than one already known physiological link, and with which we shall perhaps find more as the mysteries of our organisation, and particularly the secret workings of our nervous system, are revealed to us.

Destutt de Tracy, *De l'amour* (1813)

The love between the sexes is undoubtedly one of the first things in life and the combination of mental and physical satisfaction attained in the enjoyment of love is literally one of life's culminations. Apart from a few perverse fanatics all the world knows this and conducts life accordingly.

Sigmund Freud: Observations on Transference-Love (1915)

CONTENTS

Preface   xi

Chapter One: Life before Frieda   1

Chapter Two: Love's progress   29

Chapter Three: The road to disillusion   77

Chapter Four: New world but not so new thoughts   109

Chapter Five: A change of heart   133

Chapter Six: A propos   173

Notes   185

Index   197

Acknowledgements   202

PREFACE

Ask any reasonably literate members of the general public about Lawrence and they will tell you that his chief interest was in sex. The first thing to say is that this is not a mistake. Sex, or perhaps rather more broadly sex as it interacts with love, was a major concern for Lawrence from the beginning of his writing career. One of his closest male friends during his adolescence and early manhood was George Neville. After Lawrence's death, Neville wrote a memoir which includes a description of walking with Lawrence in the country and discussing a novel which he thinks he remembers was George Moore's *Esther Waters*. It was then that Lawrence told him that he 'wanted to write on matters of sex, but he wanted to go deeper, so very much deeper, than anybody had ever gone so far.' That this ambition should co-exist with the fact that at this stage he had almost certainly no direct, personal experience of the matter was a paradox of which he was only too painfully aware. 'Why bother with it then?', Neville asked him. 'Why bother with it?, Lawrence repeated. 'Haven't we agreed that it is the most important thing in our existence? Didn't I tell you that it is the only thing worth writing about?'[1]

When Lawrence first began to publish, the reviewers invariably complained about what seemed to many of them an obsession with sexual issues, and he began what would be a life-long battle with censorship. Yet as is suggested by the title of the novel widely regarded as his best (*Women in Love*), sex was never far in his mind from the concept of love and how the two might relate. This is true, however much his well-known, bold statement that he would 'always be the priest of love', which closely followed the completion of *Sons and Lovers*, would quickly prove to be unjustified.[2] After the First World War, and with his travels to Australia and then both New and old Mexico, his concern with love and sex temporarily took a back seat as he struggled to work out his views on politics. But it returned in full force with his last novel where Mellors is of course described as the 'lover' of Lady Chatterley and not by some other word, which would limit his role to that of a sexual partner.

Given the importance of love and sex for Lawrence in both his writing and his personal life, one might think that they would have been equally important for critics, and that anything that could be said on the subject had long ago been exhausted. If I believed this to be true, there would be no reason for writing this book. In England, the relative paucity of commentary could have something to do with the powerful direction given to Lawrence criticism as long ago as the 1950s and 1960s by F. R. Leavis. It was then that Leavis began what would prove a successful campaign to establish Lawrence as a major English writer of the 20th century, but he did so by concentrating on him as a wonderfully acute witness of the effect modern industrial society was having on individuals, and by demonstrating that, contrary to received opinion, he was not a naïve, spontaneous genius but a great artist. This was a task well worth undertaking yet one can read through all Leavis has to say on Lawrence and not be made aware that love, and sex especially, were major concerns. The situation was different in America where critics such as Mark Spilka and James Cowan began to make bold and interesting enquiries but, since their time, most of the commentary has come from two very distinct sources, if it has come at all. One of these is Feminism, and the other what is sometimes called Queer Theory. Without wanting to undervalue the illumination and challenge these have provided, it has seemed to me that there is now room, and indeed a pressing need, for a general overview of Lawrence's dealings with love and sex, undertaken in the light of Wittgenstein's suggestion that, when we are puzzled or challenged by a phenomenon, we should not seek new knowledge, but rather put into order what we already know.

This is an injunction which has to be followed in the spirit rather than the letter. The direction in which it seemed to me I did *not* want to go here is not so much towards new knowledge, but can be suggested by a sentence from the preface to a collection of essays on Lawrence's dealings with the body published in 2001 (from which I have picked up some useful suggestions). There the editor says that the items in the volume 'draw variously on French theory (Foucault, Deleuze and Guattari, Bataille, French feminism), postmodernism, Marxism, feminism and gender studies, structuralism, stylistics and narrative theory, cultural criticism and the sociology of censorship, rhetorical and myth criticism, and Freudian and Jungian psychoanalysis'.[3] Much as this might remind one of those situations that sometime occur in winter, when one has to send heavily muffled up dinner-guests back into the cold and say to them: 'Now, you're sure you haven't forgotten anything?', it indicates what often now happens to authors in academic writing: that is to say their writings are aligned, with more or less appositeness or felicity, with whatever theoretical approach from this list the commentator happens to espouse. Yet when I say that what I would like to do here instead is simply to put into order what I already know, I am very conscious that it turned out, even after many years of reading Lawrence, I did not know as much as I thought and there were therefore new things I had to find out. Nevertheless, my aim has been to set out as clearly as I can, what the obvious facts are regarding Lawrence's dealings with love and sex. It is because the resulting picture is so different from what I expected when I began the process that I thought it worth publishing, and it is certainly wildly different from what those members of that general public, to whom I began by referring, would have assumed it to be. For most of them, who may still have ringing in their ears faint echoes of the *Lady Chatterley* trial, Lawrence is the champion of sexual liberation and the passionate advocate of wholesome sexual intercourse as the key to a successful marriage or relationship. There is some justification for that view in Lawrence's life and writings, but not very much.

One possible reason for the relative lack of commentary on love and sex, but especially the latter, is that they are not the most comfortable topics for academics to discuss. This will seem a ludicrous suggestion in our liberated times, but for one thing the humour which can occasionally help to fend off the always threatening aridity of academic writing is virtually precluded here because it can so easily be taken for an indication of embarrassment. For another, the personal experience and qualifications of the author can somehow seem more in question in this context, especially if one recalls and then adapts Lawrence's own crushing remark, in his essay on Galsworthy, that 'a man with a paltry, impudent nature will never write anything but paltry, impudent criticism'.[4] What kind of person does one have to be to write about love and sex authoritatively, and at what age would it be appropriate to take the matter up given Lewis Carroll's 'You are old, Father William, the young man said / And your hair has become very white / And yet you incessantly stand on your head / Do you think, at your age, it is right?'. Yet if this is, as I believe, an important subject which needs clarifying, then there is no point in waiting for the perfectly qualified person to come along because, in that case, one might well have to wait for ever.

On a more specific level, there is the problem of vocabulary. 'Sexual intercourse' is an expression I have already used and its popular euphemistic equivalent, 'making love', is one I may from time to time find myself reduced to. There may also be occasions when I have to refer to the female genitalia. Lawrence felt that preferable to any of these expressions, and others of the same ilk, were words like 'fuck' and 'cunt', because they form 'a natural part of the mind's consciousness of the body' (whatever that is).[5] Yet his attempt to transform the way people talk about sex, radically to alter usage, has always seemed to me doomed to failure (how could one novel ever do that?); and the more limited effort with which some of the witnesses in the *Lady Chatterley* trial credited him, that is to effectively change usage merely within the confines of the novel itself, strikes me as a failure also. If that is so then my subject is increased in difficulty because of the unsatisfactory vocabulary we are stuck with.

There is a final problem which is not so much a matter of difficulty as of policy. Since putting into order what I already know about love and sex in Lawrence has surprised me, I have to assume that it will surprise others also, and in a way which is unlikely to enhance his reputation. That is a pity since one additional reason for there being so relatively little previous commentary on this aspect of Lawrence is that there is now so little commentary on him of any kind.[6] From being a super-star in the 1960s he has slipped almost entirely off the academic radar, even if his reputation outside academia has, to a certain extent, held up. This strikes me as a great pity given his remarkable gifts as a writer, and his achievements in so many areas (including those F. R. Leavis discussed). It might therefore appear the duty of any academic with an interest in these matters to do what he or she can to remedy the situation. I have to doubt this book will help to do that. Yet any worthwhile reputation has to be based on the facts as they are, and as Dr. Johnson said in a slightly different context: 'If we owe regard to the memory of the dead, there is yet more respect to be paid to knowledge, virtue and truth'.[7] Virtue is not a relevant concept in this case and although Johnson talks of truth, here that can only mean what one individual does his level best to perceive as such. Yet with those provisos, Johnson's remarks still strike me as ones to abide by and they have a more modern equivalent in Lawrence's own writing. One of his finest texts is the largely biographical introduction he wrote in 1921–2 for Maurice Magnus's *Memoirs of the Foreign Legion*. In the course of that he claims that 'the dead ask only for *justice*: not praise or exoneration … deep true justice'.[8] Inspiring words, hard though they be to live up to.

CHAPTER ONE:
LIFE BEFORE FRIEDA

SCHOPENHAUER AND JESSIE CHAMBERS

On 29 January 1906 Jessie Chambers was nineteen. As all interested parties now know, she was Lawrence's most important female companion and friend in his early years and it is significant for this topic to recall how they first got to know one another. In December 1901, when Lawrence was sixteen and working as a clerk in a surgical goods factory in Nottingham, he fell dangerously ill with pneumonia. This was only a few months after his older brother Ernest, who had been pursuing a promising business career in London, had very suddenly died. His mother was devastated by Ernest's death and must have felt that she was now threatened with another catastrophic loss. She put all her energy into caring for Lawrence, strengthening to an unusual degree whatever bond there was already between them. As he himself was aware, Lawrence's intense love for his mother had a powerful influence on his dealings with other women. When critics talk of this they invariably invoke Freud and take the story back to the time when Lawrence was a baby (as he himself does in *Sons and Lovers*). Yet a boating accident which leaves its victim with a morbid fear of water might just as well take place in adolescence as infancy. Whatever Lawrence's relations with his mother were during the Oedipal phase, the way his illness at sixteen brought the two of them closer together is likely to have been just, if not more, important.

As the crisis passed and her son began to improve, Mrs. Lawrence remembered a friend of hers, married to a man who rented a farm not many miles outside her home town of Eastwood in Nottinghamshire. She thought that the walk there, and the atmosphere of the farm itself, would be a help to her son in his convalescence. In a very short time Lawrence not only delighted in going to 'The

Haggs', as the farm was known, but endeared himself to all those who lived there. He already had a quite miraculous knowledge and appreciation of Nature which visiting the farm must have allowed him to refine and increase. His best friend was one of Jessie's brothers, Alan, but he was soon brought closer together with Jessie because she was by far the most bookish family member (like him, she would soon begin training to be a teacher). In a blatant characterisation of his relations with her in *Lady Chatterley*, Lawrence has Mellors describe how he and his first girl friend were the most 'literary-cultured couple in ten counties'.[1] When Jessie was about to turn nineteen it was natural that her brother should ask Lawrence for advice about what to buy her. He suggested a pocket-sized volume of Schopenhauer's essays, translated by Mrs. Rudolph Dircks, in what was known as 'The Scott Library'. This was typical of the books which had become available once the 1886 Education Act had began to have its effects and Britain became full of intelligent young people from the lower classes devoted to self-improvement. The heterogeneous list of volumes already published in this library, which seems to have been deliberately limited to prose, included not only English classics such as Swift, Sheridan, Shelley, Coleridge, De Quincey, Byron and Carlyle but also (in translation) Aristotle, Plato, Marcus Aurelius, Seneca, Mazzini, Heine, Montaigne, Schiller and Gogol.

Once the Schopenhauer volume was in Jessie's hands, Lawrence came over to the Haggs in order to read aloud to both her and Alan the essay in it called 'The Metaphysics of Love'. As someone who was about to become a student at Nottingham University, taking what we would now describe as a two-year teachers' training course, he was their intellectual leader and capable of translating the quotations from Latin, and other foreign languages, with which Schopenhauer's essay is littered. The essay is significant because on the question of love, and its relation to sex, Schopenhauer had a very clear answer. 'Every kind of love', he writes, close to the beginning, 'however ethereal it may seem to be, springs entirely from the instinct of sex'.[2] The 'entirely' is important and was an emphasis Lawrence would never forget. According to Jessie, the essay, and Schopenhauer generally, made a deep and powerful impression on him. Not surprisingly, one might think, given that Lawrence would go on to be the author of *Lady Chatterley's Lover*. But the situation is more complicated than it seems since what Schopenhauer meant by 'the instinct of sex' was not what we might, but rather the blind will of the species to reproduce itself. As he explains:

> Love is of such high import because it has nothing to do with the weal or woe of the present individual, as every other matter has; it has to secure the existence and special nature of the human race in future times; hence the will of the individual appears in a higher aspect as the will of the species.[3]

The advantage of this view is that it allows Schopenhauer to explain the feeling lovers often have of being in the grip of powers quite beyond their control, and the willingness they sometimes display to sacrifice their well-being, careers or even lives to the feelings they experience. It also helps him to account for the extraordinary prevalence of love as a subject in Western literature and why it is (as Schopenhauer puts it) that 'the most successful delineations of love, such, for example, as *Romeo and Juliet*, *La Nouvelle Heloïse*, and *Werther*, have achieved immortal fame'.[4] The possibilities of the topic would have long become exhausted by writers, he conjectures, were it not associated with a continuously renewable biological imperative.

Smuggled into the middle of Schopenhauer's essay is a distinction which might well have complicated his argument had he chosen to develop it. The will of the species, he suggests, is not only on a mission of self-propagation but also of self-improvement and is therefore committed to what he calls individuation. 'On the other hand,' he writes, 'mere sexual instinct is base, because without individuation, it is directed to all, and strives to preserve the species merely as regards quantity with little regard to quality'. It is quality alone which interests Schopenhauer and leads him to assert that short men always prefer big women because 'each man loves what he himself is deficient in', a confident statement which would have come as a surprise to the many ageing businessmen or rock stars who have tall, trophy wives. This pre-Darwinian parody of natural selection now seems absurd as when Schopenhauer claims that the unconscious need every one has to find a corrective to his own defects and aberrations is why 'snub-nosed persons find an aquiline nose or a parrot-like face so indescribably pleasing; and the same thing applies to every other part of the body. Men of immoderately long and attenuated build delight in a stunted and short figure'.[5] Yet Lawrence was attracted to this way of supporting one's own positions with what purported to be science and would himself do the same later when he wrote a couple of books on psychoanalysis and the unconscious. Of the two things Jessie remembered about his reading, one was that he fiercely defended, against her brother, Schopenhauer's contention that, if blonde people are attracted to the dark-skinned whereas it is rarely a case of vice-versa, it is because 'fair hair and blue eyes are a deviation from type and almost constitute an abnormality': that 'white skin is not natural to man'.[6]

The second feature of the reading Jessie remembered was more significant. Schopenhauer's logic in his essay is often difficult to follow. It is, for example, only in 'the second place' that 'every one will desire in the other individual those perfections which he himself lacks, and ... will consider imperfections which are the reverse of his own beautiful'. In the first place, he says, 'every one will ... infinitely prefer and ardently desire those who are most beautiful' (because in them 'the character of the species is most purely defined').[7] It was after reading out the phrases about ardently desiring the beautiful that Jessie remembered Lawrence had suddenly stopped and said 'That's just the trouble, though. I see what is most beautiful, and I *don't* desire it'.[8]

It seems highly probable that Jessie is retrospectively associating this moment in the reading with the crisis in her relationship with Lawrence which was to take place on Easter Monday in 1906. It was then that his family, or at least the female part of it, declared that it was unfair of him to be so constantly in Jessie's company without making it clear what his future intentions were (in 1906 Lawrence would, after all, be twenty-one). After much painful cogitation, he decided that though he felt closer to her than any other woman, he could never marry Jessie and sent her a letter which she says included the following phrases: 'What I see is the deep spirit within. That I love and can go on loving all my life. …Look, you are a nun, I give you what I would give a holy nun. So you must let me marry a woman I can kiss and embrace and make the mother of my children'.[9] Here then is a particularly clear distinction between sex and love, and what Lawrence is having to admit to himself is that, much as he liked and indeed loved Jesse, she was not sexually appealing to him. Having grown up with her (as it were), he had known her too well, over too long, for him to think of her *in that way*.

PERFECT LOVE

One obvious difficulty of talking about love and sex in Lawrence lies in the uncertain parameters of the first term. Some people love sport, lobster thermidor, moonlit evenings, but to claim that sex enters into their feelings in all these cases would mean that the issue I am discussing would have two words which were broad and vague in their meaning rather than just one. For the moment, therefore, it will be useful to limit love to what people feel for a member of the same or opposite gender who is not a close relation. It was this feeling that Schopenhauer thought could always be reduced to the instinct of sex and which in November 1909, when he was twenty-four, Lawrence declared he still knew nothing about. 'I do *not* believe in love', he wrote to Blanche Jennings, '...I never could believe in anything I do not experience'.[10]

As so often in his letters to this particular female correspondent however, Lawrence was exaggerating. Much later in his life, when he was living in Capri, he told Compton Mackenzie that the nearest he had ever come to 'perfect love' was with a young coal miner when he was about sixteen.[11] It is very likely that Mackenzie was misremembering in talking about a coal miner but that the substance of what he recalled is almost certainly accurate and Lawrence's reference must have been to Alan Chambers. 'You tell me I have no male friends', he wrote to Blanche Jennings in 1908, 'The man I have been working with in the hay [Alan Chambers] is the original of my George – lacking, alas, the other's subtlety of sympathetic discrimination which lent him his nobility. But I am very fond of my friend, and he of me. Sometimes, often, he is as gentle as a woman towards me'.[12] The person he refers to as 'my George' is one of the principal characters in Lawrence's first novel, *The White Peacock*, which he had begun writing in 1906 but which was only published at the end of 1910. The story is told by Cyril, a narrator accurately characterised by Jessie Chambers, who saw the novel through numerous drafts, as 'old-maidish'.[13] He has a high-spirited sister called Lettie who finds herself having to choose between George Saxton, the son of a local tenant farmer, for whom she has a strong physical feeling, and Leslie Tempest, whose family is rich and owns mines and who can offer her not only financial security but also a cultured milieu. The setting for much of the action is clearly the countryside round the Haggs and a major feature of the novel is nature description of quite astonishing yet at the same time somewhat stifling virtuosity. George has a sister called Emily who is clearly but also unflatteringly based on Jessie Chambers. Cyril and George are fond of each other and at one point are drying themselves after having been for a naked swim:

He saw I had forgotten to continue my rubbing, and laughing he took hold of me and began to rub me briskly, as if I were a child, or rather, a woman he loved and did not fear. I left myself quite limply in his hands, and, to get a better grip of me, he put his arm round me and pressed me against him, and the sweetness of the touch of our naked bodies one against the other was superb. It satisfied in some measure the vague, indecipherable yearning of my soul; and it was the same with him. When he had rubbed me all warm, he let me go, and we looked at each other with eyes of still laughter, and our love was perfect for a moment, more perfect than any love I have known since, either for man or woman.[14]

The degree of intimacy here is not entirely unexpected. In a passage which was finally deleted from the published version Cyril tells George 'See, I've fallen in love with you, my Jonathan'; but in another, which survives, he walks into the farm house where the Saxtons are living and finds George reading: 'He looked up as I entered, and I loved him when he looked at me, as he lingered on his quiet 'Hello!' His eyes were beautifully eloquent – as eloquent as a kiss.'[15]

It seems incredible that Lawrence could have written phrases and passages like the ones above without being consciously aware of their implications; but to show that he almost certainly did, it is worth going back to the memoir of George Neville. He was aggressively heterosexual and well known as a womaniser (his eventual fate in that regard would furnish Lawrence with material for one of his novels). He stresses continually his own knowledge of women as opposed to Lawrence's ignorance, but in his memoir recalls an occasion when, irritated by his friend's inability to draw convincing pictures of the male body, took off all his clothes in order to demonstrate what a real man looked like. He also claims that the bathing scene in *The White Peacock* was based on an episode in his own relationship with its author.[16] This is perfectly possible: though the model for George was (as Lawrence himself says) Alan Chambers, it may well have been Neville with whom he went swimming. What is interesting, however, is the unself-conscious way in which someone like Neville, with a reputation to keep up, could lay claim to involvement in it. This suggests that, like his more famous friend, he could see nothing in the episode beyond the bounds of what young men usually feel and do.

In early 1915 Lawrence was visited by E. M. Forster, an avowed although not a practising homosexual. Shortly afterwards Forster urged a correspondent to read the chapter in *The White Peacock* called 'A Poem of Friendship' (the one in which the bathing epi-sode occurs) because it was 'most beautiful'. 'The whole book is the queerest product of subconsciousness I have yet struck', he went on, ' – he has not a glimmering from first to last of what he is up to'.[17] It is untrue that, in general, Lawrence did not know what he was up to in *The White Peacock*; but he seems to have written about Cyril and George without realising that there could be any homo-sexual feeling involved. As he left his own environment and began to mix with a slightly bohemian writers' group in London, and even more as he became acquainted with members of what became known as Bloomsbury, he was helped to take a more accurate view of his own feelings. But if one goes back to 1906 and his discovery that he had no sexual feeling for Jessie Chambers, and then link this with what Cyril says about George, whom Lawrence is clear was modelled on her brother, it might seem reasonable to suggest – as did one or two of his contemporaries at the time and the oc-casional commentator much later – that Lawrence was essentially homosexual and that the clue to his writings about love and sex lies in his struggles either to repress or adapt to that fact.

DEALING WITH FRUSTRATION

The most obvious objection to the idea that Lawrence was a re-pressed homosexual is the evidence everywhere in his writing that he was strongly attracted, not only to the bodies of men but also to those of women (although in 1906, not to that of Jessie Chambers). There are descriptions in his writing, some of which will be quoted later, which make it quite clear that it was not just intellectual cu-riosity that made him more and more desperate to find a woman to sleep with him after he had turned twenty (he would have to wait until he was twenty-four). At the beginning of a whole book on love (*De l'amour*) which the French novelist Stendhal wrote in the 1820s, and which Lawrence read, there is a list of the different forms love can take. Third on that list is what Stendhal calls *amour physique* which he describes as follows:

> While out hunting, finding a beautiful and fresh peasant girl who flees into the woods. Everyone is familiar with the love based on this kind of pleasure; however desiccated and unhappy one's character, that's how one starts off at sixteen.[18]

In the late-Victorian or Edwardian Eastwood of Lawrence's day, peasant girls of this variety were in short supply. The result in his case was a build-up of sexual frustration which he is very good at describing in his early fiction, especially in *Sons and Lovers*. It was a subject which had hardly ever been broached directly by previous novelists, although Thomas Hardy had made some moves in that direction in *Jude the Obscure*, a work Lawrence knew well. There is a strong sense of personal understanding when, in *The Study of Thomas Hardy* which Lawrence wrote in 1914, he talks of the mis-take Jude makes in insisting on having sex with Sue Bridehead:

Now he wants that which is necessary for him if he is to go on. He wants, at its lowest, the physical, sexual relief. For continually baulked sexual desire, or necessity, makes a man unable to live freely, scotches him, stultifies him. And where a man is roused to the fullest pitch, as Jude was roused by Sue, then the principal connection becomes a necessity, if only for relief.[19]

Relief is what, in *Sons and Lovers*, Paul Morel cries out for in order not to be scotched or stultified.

Perhaps the clearest illustrations of how seriously Lawrence suffered from sexual frustration in his early days can be found in his poetry rather than his prose. 'Virgin Youth' is a prime example and remarkable enough to deserve quoting in full:

> Now and again
> All my body springs alive,
> And the life that is polarised in my eyes,
> That quivers between my eyes and mouth,
> Flies like a wild thing across my body,
> Leaving my eyes half-empty and clamorous,
> Filling my still breasts with a flush and a flame,
> Gathering the soft ripples below my breasts
> Into urgent, passionate waves,
> And my soft, slumbering belly
> Quivering awake with one impulse of desire,
> Gathers itself fiercely together;
> And my docile, fluent arms
> Knotting themselves with wild strength
> To clasp – what they have never clasped.
> Then I tremble, and go trembling
> Under the wild, strange tyranny of my body,
> Till it has spent itself,
> And the relentless nodality of my eyes reasserts itself,

Till the bursten flood of life ebbs back to my eyes,
Back from my beautiful, lonely body
Tired and unsatisfied.[20]

Whether or not this is a good poem, it is an exceptional one given the year in which it was written. This was 1909, when Lawrence was twenty-four. 'Virgin Youth' was not published until 1916, in a collection called *Amores*, but that he should have published it at all shows the extent to which, by that date, he was willing to expose himself since the poem is so inescapably and revealingly autobiographical. Writing to Edward Garnett in 1912 about his second novel, *The Trespasser*, Lawrence said he had begun to loathe the book because it meant exposing his 'most palpitant, sensitive self' to others; and he went on to conjecture that Stendhal must have 'writhed in torture every time he remembered *Le rouge et le noir* was public property'.[21] There are reasons which will become clear later why, by 1916, Lawrence was no longer so sensitive about exposing himself to others; but that he did so repeatedly would seem to make a biographical approach to his writings difficult to avoid. As F. R. Leavis once wisely said, 'There are some writers a serious interest in whose work leads inevitably to a discussion of their personalities'; and towards the start of *D. H. Lawrence: Novelist* he wrote, 'it is impossible to study the work and art [of Lawrence] without forming a vivid sense of the man, and touching on the facts of his history'.[22] Not that Leavis was less aware than others of the pitfalls of biographical reading, or the dangers of simple one-to-one equivalences, and these are in fact well illustrated in Lawrence's own critical practice where he has a strong tendency to suppose that the main character in a fiction must be a portrait of its author (his otherwise splendid review of Thomas Mann's *Death in Venice* would be a case in point).[23]

'Virgin Youth' is one of many poems which Lawrence rewrote substantially when in 1928 he was preparing his *Collected Poems*. Then he made it crystal clear that the description of his 'soft slumbering belly / Quivering awake with one impulse of desire' had indicated an erection; yet in 1916 it would have been hard for an alert reader to mistake it for anything else, just as that same imaginary reader must have understood the reference to the body spending itself, and the 'bursten flood of life', as an allusion to either spontaneous emission or the consequences of masturbation.

Masturbation is the simplest of temporary solutions to the problem of sexual frustration, an obvious answer to that need for relief which Lawrence refers to when he talks of Hardy's Jude; but it was one which was very probably denied to him by both his background and his temperament. If there is no direct evidence of this in the writing – apart from suggestions of the kind one finds in 'Virgin Youth' – it is because the practice, and the feelings which ensue, were virtually impossible to dramatise in his day. (Censorship, of both the formal and informal variety, is an important factor which needs always to be borne in mind when discussing Lawrence's writings on love and sex.) Much later than either the composition or first publication of this poem however, in *Fantasia of the Unconscious*, which appeared after the war, he imagines a rather bluff parent telling a son who has just arrived at puberty that he ought to leave himself alone, that he knows erections will keep coming on him at night, but that he must not go creeping off by himself and doing things 'on the sly'. 'Probably I've behaved more foolishly and perniciously than ever you will', the father is imagined as saying; yet the boy must not have secret thoughts but try and be 'manly' and quiet in himself.[24] Shortly before he died, Lawrence came round to discussing the issue in more detail. This was in an essay on pornography and obscenity where he attacks the former as an 'invariable stimulant to the vice of self-abuse, onanism, masturbation, call it what you like'. There are some, he notes, who defend masturbation as a solution to an 'otherwise insoluble sex problem'. Yet while in the young a certain amount of masturbation is inevitable, it is not therefore natural: 'I think', he writes, perhaps recalling his own youth, 'there is no boy or girl who masturbates without feeling a sense of shame, anger, and futility'. For him, therefore, masturbation is 'the most dangerous sexual vice a society can be afflicted with, in the long run'. This is because in sexual intercourse, 'even in the homosexual intercourse', there is a give and take, reciprocity, whereas in masturbation there is what is known as a 'dead loss', a null effect which leaves one – in the words he had used in the last line of 'Virgin Youth' – 'tired and unsatisfied'. It is an activity where there is 'no real object, there is only subject'.[25]

NARCISSUS

The remarks concerning self-enclosure, which in his pornography and obscenity essay Lawrence claims is exacerbated by masturbation, belong to his later years; but it was a tendency in himself he was aware of from early on. In 'Virgin Youth', the willingness he shows to exhibit all the nuances of his own feelings means that he is able to indicate that this state is not without its pleasures. That in the penultimate line the bursten flood leaves his body not only lonely but 'beautiful' is suggestive of a narcissism which hovers around the poem as a whole. Delight in his own physique is expressed in a number of his early writings: in the poem 'The Wild Common', for example, or in the short story 'Love among the Haystacks' where Maurice, one of the two male protagonists, decides to wash his whole naked body in the open air and relishes the 'soft touches and caresses' of the breeze on his sides, the way the meadow-sweet 'touched his thighs', and also feels that he had 'never known the wonder in himself as before'.[26] Any doubt that feelings like this were also the writer's is dispelled by an early letter Lawrence wrote to Blanche Jennings in which he described how, after working in the fields of the Chambers farm with Alan, he felt himself 'fairly strong' and 'pretty well developed':

> Indeed, as I was rubbing myself down in the late twilight
> a few minutes ago, and as I passed my hands over my sides
> where the muscles are suave and secret, I did love myself.
> I am thin, but well skimmed over with muscle; my skin is
> white and unblemished; soft and dull with a fine pubes-
> cent bloom, not shiny like my friend's. I am very fond of
> myself.[27]

This was written at the end of July 1908, six weeks before Lawrence's
twenty-third birthday and demonstrates, even more startlingly than
his poetry or fiction, how willing he was to articulate everything he
felt. Later, he would recognise how his self-enclosing narcissism
was closely associated with solipsism, the tendency, which is particularly evident in writers (Wordsworth being a good example), to
regard the world as a mere extension of self.

There is a further association here which may seem legitimate
in Lawrence's case and this is with the rampant anthropomorphism
that disfigures some of his early Nature writing. *The Trespasser* was
based on an account of a doomed love affair given to him by Helen
Corke, a woman who taught in Croydon when he was also employed in a school there. Her married violin teacher had deserted
his family to spend a holiday with Corke on the Isle of Wight, but
had committed suicide on his return home. Lawrence's rendering
of these unhappy events, and of the holiday period especially, is
another virtuoso exercise in poetic prose and contains many paragraphs like the following which describes the male protagonist,
who is called Siegmund, walking alone down to the sea for his
morning swim:

> The morning was exceedingly fair, and it looked at him so
> gently, that his blue eyes trembled with self-pity. A frag-
> ment of scarlet geranium glanced up at him as he passed,
> so that amid the vermilion tyranny of the uniform it wore,
> he could see the eyes of the flower, wistful, offering him

love, as one sometimes sees the eyes of a man beneath the
brass helmet of a soldier, and is startled. Everything looked
at him with the same eyes of tenderness, offering him, tim-
idly, a little love.[28]

That the eyes of the flower should be compared with those of a
soldier is a detail which will become relevant later in my account,
but the general habit the passage displays is common enough in
Lawrence's early work, especially his poetry. A typical example is
called 'Weeknight Service', and describes the 'silver moon' as being
'up there in the sky / Serenely smiling at naught', while 'patient
Night / Sits indifferent, hugged in her rags', and 'the wise old trees
/ Drop their leaves with a faint, sharp hiss of contempt'.[29] The general effect is of a man purporting to describe the outside world but
always in fact talking about himself.

    This weakness is one which could be dismissed as no more than
a question of style, especially as Lawrence's descriptions of Nature
are otherwise so impressive; but that it is not what one is prompted
to think by the way he himself eventually became highly conscious
of it. In the collection *Look! We Have Come Through!*, which records
the early days of his relationship with Frieda Weekley, the woman
who in 1914 would become his wife, there is a poem entitled 'New
Heaven and Earth'. This expresses very powerfully the nausea he
felt in being trapped in a world of his own imaginings where everything was, as he memorably puts it, 'tainted' with himself: 'skies,
trees, flowers, water, … it was all tainted with myself, I knew it all
to start with because it was all myself'. What has saved him from
this situation, he says, is touching the side of his wife in bed and
realising that there was something in the world which was 'ver-
ily … not me'.[30] In a more decorous or puritanical age, it was a
wall or tree which Wordsworth remembered having to grab hold
of as a child in order to save himself from solipsism, or what he
describes, in a famous autobiographical note to the Immortality
Ode, as an 'abyss of idealism'. That for Lawrence it was the body of

a woman is further help in explaining why he was later so hostile to the self-enclosure of masturbation, and came to feel it was 'the most dangerous sexual vice a society can be afflicted with'. Only in sexual intercourse, he believed, could one escape the self and be released into a recognition of one's own identity in relation to other people. But this was a heavy burden to put on the sexual act, and why it did not always happen, and what dangers one ran in trying to make it happen, were (as I shall show) questions that would remain to torment him.

Prostitution

In the year after Stendhal published his book on love, William Hazlitt wrote what could be described as its English, lower middle-class equivalent (although he gave it an upper-class title). *Liber Amoris* painfully and embarrassingly records Hazlitt's infatuation with his landlord's second daughter, Sarah Walker, who allowed him certain liberties but steadfastly refused to let him go any further. The consequence was a good deal of sexual frustration which Hazlitt assuaged by sending out for a prostitute whom Sarah would then direct to his room. He could do this because sex as a biological need was separated in his mind from love (as it was also in Stendhal's). This was a more difficult procedure for Lawrence to perform and although there are indications that he may sometimes have thought of visiting a prostitute, there is no proof that he ever did so, or that he felt this would be any more of a satisfactory solution to the sexual frustration from which he was suffering than masturbation would be.

It is in the description of Tom Brangwen's adolescence and young manhood in *The Rainbow* that the problem of prostitution for anyone brought up as Tom (and Lawrence) had been, is treated in most detail. There is a moment there when Tom gets drunk in a public house and goes upstairs with a prostitute 'who seduced him'.

The relevant passage contains too much that is striking not to be quoted with only minor omissions:

> The thing was something of a shock to him. In the close intimacy of the farm kitchen, the woman occupied the supreme position. The men deferred to her in the house, on all household points, on all points of morality and behaviour. The woman was the symbol for that further life which comprised religion and love and morality. The men placed in her hands their own conscience, they said to her 'Be my conscience-keeper, be the angel at the doorway, guarding my outgoing and incoming.' …They depended on her for their stability. Without her, they would have felt like straws in the wind, to be blown hither and thither at random. She was the anchor and the security, she was the restraining hand of God, at times highly to be execrated.
>
> Now when Tom Brangwen, at nineteen, a youth fresh like a plant, rooted in his mother and sister, found that he had lain with a prostitute woman in a common public-house, he was very much startled. For him, there was until that time only one kind of woman – his mother and his sister.[31]

The Rainbow is an ambitious novel. It aims to show, through the history of a representative family, how the feelings and attitudes of the English were altered by the transition from an agricultural to an industrial society in the nineteenth century, and in particular what effect this had on women. The acuteness of the analysis in this passage seems less startling now than it must have done at the time because there have been, in the intervening period, so many sociologically-inclined studies of 'the angel in the house'. Here what the description of the role of women in Tom's life does is provide one possible explanation of why he can find his encounter with a prostitute so disheartening. The experience is for Tom a shock and puts fear in his heart. Apart from the 'paralysed horror when he felt he might have taken a disease', there is above all the disappointment that the whole thing had amounted to so little. 'It had been so nothing, so dribbling and functional, that he was ashamed to expose himself to the risk of a repetition of it' (although he does).[32]

Yet what Tom Brangwen cannot principally work out is what he feels about the women who provide the moral authority in his household (and whom he respects), and the prostitute he sleeps with. It is on that topic that Freud had published in 1910 a well-known article which in its translated version is usually known as 'On the Universal Tendency to Debasement in the Sphere of Love'. This begins with the problem of 'psychical impotence' in men whose natures are strongly libidinous and traces their difficulties back to their failure to reconcile the affectionate with the sensual currents in their natures: 'Where they love they do not desire and where they desire they do not love'. The respectable women with whom they are associated, or to whom they are married, remind them too much of their mothers and sisters, who themselves are the objects of heavily repressed incestuous feelings. To fully express their sexual natures they need to find women who are socially degraded, or whom they themselves are able to degrade with 'perverse' practices.[33]

Characteristically suggestive and ingenious, Freud's short essay is often associated with Lawrence although working out just how relevant it is to him, in (for example) any consideration of his long relationship with Jessie Chambers, is not easy. Having made it clear that he could not marry her because she was not the kind of girl with whom he could imagine himself doing what was necessary to have children, he did not break off the relationship but looked around among his female colleagues in Croydon for someone who was willing to provide him with sex without the assurance of marriage. Having drawn a number of blanks (Helen Corke perhaps being among them), he convinced himself that he loved Jessie after all and in 1909 asked her to sleep with him. Given what this

meant to her in the social atmosphere of the time, she was naturally reluctant but yielded to his insistence because she loved and
admired him so much. The understanding was that if their coming together was a success, it would naturally lead on to marriage.
When Lawrence decided it was not, he broke with Jessie again, although on this occasion more definitively. It was about this period
that George Neville claims to have told him that buying oneself a
woman (going to a prostitute) was much better, and by implication
more moral, than trading on the regard of a girl friend without that
regard being properly reciprocated.[34] Looking at the way Lawrence
dealt with this episode later in his writing, it is hard to avoid the
conclusion that Neville was right.

JESSIE AGAIN

In *The White Peacock*, Lawrence transposed much of his own experience into a genteel, middle-class environment, almost certainly
because he felt that this would make the novel more acceptable to
the largely middle-class reading public. In *The Trespasser* he used
as a base the experiences of his friend Helen Corke; but when he
came back to situations which were in essence autobiographical,
in the first drafts of what would become *Sons and Lovers*, Jessie
Chambers did him (and the world) an immense favour by saying
that he ought to stick much closer to what he himself had seen and
known. One cruelly ironic consequence was that Lawrence decided
to dramatise his failed sexual encounters with her. These appear in
the chapter which in the final version of the novel is called 'The
Test on Miriam' (the name he often used for Jessie). As very many
commentators have noted, this is a scandalous title since whatever
test there was applies just as much to the male protagonist (Paul
Morel) as to his female partner.

The first part of this chapter is nevertheless sufficiently well
written to make the reader understand and even sympathise with
Paul's efforts to persuade Miriam to sleep with him, and describes

very well how the inhibitions she feels as a lover partly derive from
her discomfort with the idea of sexual intercourse outside marriage. At one point the two of them have the cottage of a relative to
themselves for the day and are able to make love in some comfort:

> He never forgot seeing her as she lay naked on the bed,
> when he was unfastening his collar. First he saw only her
> beauty, and was blind with it. She had the most beauti-
> ful hips he had ever imagined. He stood unable to move
> or speak, looking at her, his face half smiling with won-
> der. And then he wanted her, and threw off his things.
> And then, as he went forward to her, her hands lifted in a
> little pleading movement, and he looked at her face, and
> stopped. Her big brown eyes were watching him, still and
> resigned and loving; she lay as if she had given herself up
> to sacrifice: there was her body for him; but the look at the
> back of her eyes, like a creature awaiting immolation, ar-
> rested him, and all his blood fell back.[35]

When this paragraph was first published the informal censorship
of Lawrence's friend Edward Garnett meant that there was no 'naked' in the first sentence, and no reference to Miriam's hips or Paul
throwing off his things. In 1913 it was still, however, a bold treatment of a difficult subject and yet another example of Lawrence's
willingness to risk self-exposure, the public display of events related to his most intimate experiences, although in this particular
case, and with Jessie Chambers in mind, one must also say that the
paragraph illustrates his often cruel indifference to what one could
call collateral damage. But the words he uses here make the dilemma of Miriam and Paul clear so that the uncomfortable and
unpleasant part of the chapter only comes after Paul has decided
that, since only one or two of their several encounters have been
pleasurable for him, he must bring an end to the relationship. Naturally distraught, Miriam tells him that he has always been fighting

her off and Paul takes this as a denial of what had been genuine between them, that she had 'really played with him, not he with her'.[36] In this curious and unconvincing fashion, he shifts all the blame for the failure of the relationship onto her.

It is not known quite what version of 'The Test on Miriam' Jessie saw. Lawrence had shown her the chapter before the final re-writing of *Sons and Lovers*, completed while he was living with Frieda Weekley in Italy, so that his treatment of his sexual relationship with her may have been a little different from what we now read in the novel. Whatever it was, it offended her deeply and she never communicated with him again. The chapter itself would have been bad enough, but just as hurtful might have been what comes before. There, built up in effective scene after effective scene, there is an analysis of the kind of person Lawrence had concluded Jessie had become which is one of the major strengths of the novel. Deeply serious and intense, unable to take anything lightly, self-doubting but paradoxically rigid in her beliefs, Miriam Leivers is always ready for self-sacrifice but also subconsciously aware of how renunciation can be a method for securing what she most wants. It is no wonder that her presence can sometimes weigh heavily on Paul Morel who has a light-hearted as well as a (very occasional) irresponsible aspect to his nature, and that the integration of an explicitly sexual element into their long-standing, loving relationship should prove so difficult for them both. Whatever form this analysis took in the novel Jessie saw it would have been hard to accept, and even harder would have been what she probably found in a poem which was written shortly after the end of their physical relationship but when Lawrence was still maintaining the habit, established over many years, of sending everything he wrote to her. This was first called 'Last Words to Muriel' (one of his alternative names for Jessie) but then 'Last Words to Miriam' and it as such it appeared in his 1916 collection *Amores*. The poem does at least begin by acknowledging his share in the responsibility for what had happened when they had slept with one another:

> Yours is the shame and sorrow,
> But the disgrace is mine;

although quite why Jessie should have felt 'shame' is not clear. Lawrence talks then of the 'balk' he had suffered in exploring her body, and the way the evident pain she suffered 'broke / My fine, craftsman's nerve' (a reference too insufferably crass to require comment). 'You are shapely, you are adorned', he says 'But opaque and dull in the flesh'. He has tried but failed to remedy this opacity and this dullness through sexual intercourse and wonders what her fate will now be:

> Now who will burn you free
> From your body's terrors and dross,
> Since the fire has failed in me?
> What man will stoop in your flesh to plough
> The shrieking cross?[37]

This last reference is obscure: perhaps, given its subject matter, it was not meant to be understood fully. Ploughing is clearly a reference to copulation, and the context suggests that the shrieking needs to be attributed to Miriam for whom sex has been akin to a crucifixion; yet there seems to be some biblical reference lurking in the background that would make everything more precise. Whether or not that is so, the poem as a whole is remarkably unpleasant and, as far as Jessie Chambers is concerned, must have seemed just as much a matter for deep resentment as 'The Test on Miriam'.

Jessie Chambers was a young woman who had already had a lot to put up with. She must have recognised herself as the model for Emily Saxton in *The White Peacock* and, for most of that novel, she is represented as recessive, a little prim and – in a characteristic which is given to Miriam Leivers in *Sons and Lovers* and which we know from letters particularly irritated Lawrence – given to extravagant expressions of smothering emotion over children, small

animals and flowers. It is therefore a complete surprise when the
narrator of *The White Peacock* begins to respond just a little to her
evident devotion to him and even, in the penultimate chapter, refers
to her as his 'old sweetheart'.[38] Whatever inconsistencies in characterisation all this might involve, there is a much more surprising
one earlier on. For all its lushness, *The White Peacock* has some very
effective scenes. These mostly occur when Lawrence is dramatis-
ing the unhappy marriages of his two central figures (his home
background seems to have made him an expert on the subject); but
there is one where George and others are chasing rabbits in a field
in order to wring their necks. Emily expresses fastidious disgust
at this behaviour but later, after her farm has been having trouble
with a couple of wild dogs which are on the loose and doing great
damage, there is a scene where the narrator comes across her just after she has finished killing one of these dogs with her bare hands.[39]
This seems impossibly out of character for this Emily, but not for a
real person with the same first name whom Lawrence would have
read about in Mrs. Gaskell's biography of Charlotte Brontë. The
descriptions there of how brutally Emily Brontë dealt with her dog
when it became unruly would stick in anyone's mind.[40] The collo-
cation is a reminder of the extent to which *Wuthering Heights* is one
of the texts lurking in the background to *The White Peacock*, with
George Saxton as a kind of watered-down Heathcliff; but also of
the fact that, although Lawrence often relied on his personal experience when writing, some of those who provided models were not
people he had actually known but rather figures he had met with
in books. True as this is, the degree of consolation which it might
have provided Jessie Chambers as she read through what Lawrence
had made of his long relationship with her can only ever have been
slight.

CLARA DAWES

Although Jessie Chambers was in no doubt that in 'The Test on Miriam' Lawrence was describing what had happened between them, she of course interpreted the episodes quite differently. In her view, the blame for the general failure of her relationship with Lawrence lay principally with his mother. Setting aside the fact of her very natural apprehension about extra-marital sex, that *both* parties were very probably virgins, and that Lawrence had previously decided that he could not find Jessie sexually attractive, her remarks might lead one back to Freud if it were not that all she seems to have meant by them was that Mrs. Lawrence did not like her and was unduly possessive. The first charge is true and the second could have been although it might also have been the case that Lawrence's mother viewed the long intimacy between her so evidently talented son and Jessie with disapproval because she felt that too early a marriage, or an unexpected pregnancy, would frustrate the keen ambition she had to see him get on in the world. In *Sons and Lovers* Lawrence may have heightened the contrast between the mother and Paul's first girl friend for dramatic effect, with the former a hard-headed, sensible sometimes satirical Puritan and the latter so single-mindedly soulful, yearning and romantic that the idea she may 'absorb' him is made to seem entirely credible.

Lawrence's mother died in December 1910, and just before her death, when it was very clear she had not long to live, he became engaged. The young woman to whom he proposed was not then Jessie Chambers but someone who had begun training as a teacher in Eastwood when he had, and to whom he had always been physically attracted. Only when he knew he would soon no longer have his mother, an incipiently Freudian argument might run, was he able to attach himself to another woman although one potential flaw in it is that, although only three days before his mother's death Lawrence claimed that she would rise from her grave to stop him marrying Jessie, she did approve of Louie Burrows, if only after some initial reluctance.[41] This bears indirectly on the literary critical problem as to whether, in reading *Sons and Lovers*, one assumes that Mrs. Morel would never have let her son go or that she is simply demonstrating a mother's natural anxiety not to see him commit himself to a woman she instinctively knows to be unsuitable.

Lawrence had previously been looking for sex without being tied down, but better to marry than to burn, as St. Paul says. The problem was that Louie Burrows was the kind of women for whom pre-marital sex was unthinkable, and the governing social conventions about how much money a couple needed to save before they married meant that the engagement would have to be a long one. The result was that Lawrence burned even more. It was during this period, that he again tried to persuade Helen Corke that she should sleep with him without feeling that he would need to break his engagement to Louie in order for her to do so. This was a time also of course when Lawrence was not only a school teacher but a promising young writer who frequented a literary set in London that included Ford Madox Hueffer, Ezra Pound as well as other writers now less well known. These were people who held views on sexual behaviour very different from those he had known at home. George Neville describes how on one occasion when Lawrence was with Louie in her home, she took his jacket out onto the lawn in order to brush it and a number of condoms fell out. He seems to have kept these in case he decided to try a prostitute, had some luck with Helen Corke, or his landlady in Croydon, and he would certainly have used them when he slept with Jessie. But what the strait-laced Louie would have felt about them, Neville fails to make clear.[42]

Masturbation, prostitution, a willing girl friend were all solutions to sexual frustration which Lawrence either tried or did not think possible; but there was a fourth which was the dissatisfied married woman. In Eastwood, Alice Dax was one of these. Unsatisfactorily married to a local chemist, she was an unconventional

woman with strong feminist views. She seems to have been attracted to Lawrence, identified his need, and quite deliberately chosen
to supply it. Without the brief affair she had with him, it is unlikely
that the description in *Sons and Lovers* of how Paul Morel gets to
know Clara Dawes and then sleeps with her in the chapter which
follows immediately 'The Test on Miriam' (an experiment Clara has
encouraged), would not have the form it does. Certainly the early
details about Clara's involvement in the women's movement would
seem to come from Dax, although she was not separated from her
husband as Clara is. But her feminism rather fades away in the
later scenes of the novel which are striking for their eroticism. After
observing her 'beautiful figure', for example, the sexually frustrated
Paul spends an uncomfortable weekend in desperate anticipation
of being able to move closer to it. She has a 'soft down' on her face
that he wants to touch; and 'the heaviness of a very full ear of corn
that dips slightly in the wind'. When he puts his arm around her
'his fingertips felt the rocking of her breast' and later, when he sees
her naked, he notices that 'her breasts were heavy'.[43] There is in fact
hardly a physical description of Clara in which her breasts are not
mentioned and in phrases that are not those of a homosexual who,
in a Proustian fashion, is transposing features that attract him in a
young man on to a female figure. According to Jessie Chambers,
that figure was not solely based on Dax but was an amalgam of
several of the women Lawrence knew, including Louie Burrows.
But since the descriptions of actual sexual intercourse we now have
were written after Lawrence had met and was living with Frieda
Weekley, she is no doubt a contributor to the writing also, especially as the phrases I have quoted suggest someone built as she
was rather than the tall, somewhat angular Alice Dax of the photographs which still survive.

   Paul and Clara often make love in the open air so that, in a
well-known assertion in the novel, 'they had met, and included
in their meeting the thrust of the manifold grass stems, the cry
of the pewits, the wheel of the stars'.[44] He at least had completely

lost himself on that particular occasion, given himself up to those forces Schopenhauer talks about, with the crucial difference that the German philosopher, in his pessimism, regards these as indifferent to individual life so that sex which in itself may be a triumphant experience might just as well leave one with 'a hateful companion for life' rather than a person one could enjoy living with.[45] For Lawrence, these forces are not so much from God as manifestations of the Godhead itself ('God doesn't *know* things, he is things' says Paul at one moment),[46] and can thus not be anything other than beneficent. Thanks to Clara, Paul is able to experience the impersonality of passion as if both of them 'had been the blind agents of a great force', but a force which one needs must respect and honour.[47] But it is here that Lawrence runs up against one of the many paradoxes, or even contradictions, in the view of the significance and importance of sexual intercourse he was beginning to elaborate. On one of the mornings after they have made love, Paul reflects that his coming together with Clara 'had happened because of her, but it was not her … He felt more and more that his experience had been impersonal and not Clara'. Yet that she may have just happened to be a means to an end, has not escaped Clara's notice either. When she voices her complaints, she says it as if 'I hadn't got you – as if all of you weren't there – and as if it weren't *me* you were taking' and asks 'is it *me* you want, or is it *It*?'. She is not convinced by his suggestion that sex is something in which their intimacy naturally culminates.[48] Thus if intercourse has the advantage of putting Paul in touch with impersonal forces, so that he becomes an impersonal force himself and is therefore an essentially religious experience, it also appears to make his partner feel that she is being used. Lawrence will struggle with this difficulty all his writing career.

And there is another problem with his developing views which begins to surface as he describes the experience of Paul and Clara. After an episode in which Paul again feels he has merged with the impersonality of Nature, Lawrence writes that 'they did not often reach again the height of that once when the pewits had called. Gradually some mechanical effort spoiled their loving, or, when they had splendid moments, they had them separately and not so satisfactorily'. It is because of this that they slowly begin 'to introduce novelties, to get back some of the feeling of satisfaction',[49] including making love close to where people are passing. The difficulty is how to combine those privileged moments when the sex seems to justify the heavy weight of significance which has been placed on it with a long-term relationship. Perhaps, however, he already has the beginnings of at least one answer in the episode where Paul is discussing with Miriam Clara's marriage with the husband from whom she is separated and comparing the relations she has had with him to those of his own parents. 'Yes', he says, 'but my mother, I believe, got *real* joy and satisfaction out of my father, at first. I believe she had a passion for him'. And he goes on:

> That's what one *must have*, ... the real, real flame of feeling through another person, once, only once, if it only last three months. See, my mother looks as if she'd *had* everything for her living and developing. There's not a tiny bit of a feeling of sterility about her.[50]

The buried metaphor here would seem to be fertilisation but the implication is that sexual intercourse does not have to keep on being significant if it has once been so, although what it then becomes, or why one should then go on with it, poses another set of problems.

CHAPTER TWO:
LOVE'S PROGRESS

COUP DE FOUDRE

Lawrence's affair with Alice Dax began while he was still engaged to Louie Burrows but, about a year after his mother's death, a serious illness had led the doctors to decide that he was threatened with consumption and forced him to take time off work. It was while he was convalescing in Bournemouth that he decided he would not go back to school teaching but instead risk trying to make his way as a professional writer. That this meant he would have no reliable, steady income, and therefore be unable to save up to be married, was perhaps not the only reason he then felt he had for breaking with Louie, although he always remained fond of her. If she was in the future only a minor source of guilt, it was because she was overshadowed by Jessie Chambers as a major one.

The affair with Alice Dax would no doubt have gone on after these events had she not been superseded by another dissatisfied wife, although one who was perhaps less angrily so. Having decided to give up his secure job, Lawrence was considering going to Germany as a language assistant, to gain new experiences, have more time for his writing and at least earn *something*. He therefore decided to seek the help of Professor Ernest Weekley, the man who had taught him French and German when he was at what is now Nottingham University. In early March, he went to visit Weekley at his house in a prosperous area of Nottingham and had lunch with both him and his wife.

The meeting with Frieda Weekley broke not just the sexual but also the emotional log-jam for Lawrence. 'Whoever loved that loved not at first sight' says Phoebe in *As You Like It* and both Romeo and Juliet would have agreed. The French call this experience the *coup de foudre* and there seems little doubt that, for the first time in his life, that is what Lawrence experienced. It was not long before he was calling Frieda 'the most wonderful woman in all England'.[1] There are not many treatments of the *coup de foudre* in Lawrence's fiction, but there are some, although they hardly accord to the conventional type. When Gudrun first sees Gerald Crich in the opening chapter of *Women in Love*, for example, she thinks to herself 'I shall know more of that man' and wonders 'Am I *really* singled out for him in some way?' Connie Chatterley's glimpse of Mellors washing himself in his back yard is an epiphany for her;[2] but the clearest example here is in *The Rainbow* with Tom Brangwen's first sight of Lydia Lensky as he is taking a load of seed back to his farm, and walking alongside his horse:

> She had heard the cart, and looked up. Her face was pale and clear, she had thick dark eyebrows and a wide mouth, curiously held. He saw her face clearly, as if by a light in the air. He saw her face so distinctly, that he ceased to coil on himself, and was suspended.
>   'That's her', he said involuntarily. As the cart passed by, splashing through the thin mud, she stood back against the bank. Then, as he walked still besides his britching horse, his eyes met hers. He looked quickly away, pressing back his head, a pain of joy running through him. He could not bear to think of anything.[3]

There is a context for this encounter which helps to explain it (as there is of course for Connie's glimpse of Mellors washing). Lydia is Polish, and earlier in *The Rainbow* Tom has had a brief meeting with a foreigner which has intrigued and fascinated him with a suggestion of ways of life entirely different from those he has always known. All his previous attempts to find a satisfactory sexual partner have ended in failure so that, subconsciously at least, he could be described as on the lookout for one. It is nonetheless important that his 'That's her' is involuntary, even if much less so than Romeo's words when he first sees Juliet. Romeo's case is more distinctly Schopenhaurean, a matter of being prepared by Nature, or by biology, for falling suddenly in love rather than by any previous, *social* experiences.

Yet that Tom Brangwen can be accurately thought of as 'falling in love' when he first sees Lydia, rather than instinctively recognising in her someone who could fulfil his needs, is perhaps a little dubious, even if 'love' is a word Lawrence himself was at first happy to use without inhibitions after meeting Frieda, and then fairly rapidly sleeping with her. The state of inflamed need which sexual frustration can sometimes engender in young men, especially as they reach their early twenties, is attributed to Maurice in that early Lawrence story already mentioned, 'Love among the Haystacks', and to his brother Geoffrey, who is a year older. It tells how both of them find female partners during a night in late summer when Maurice is guarding his father's haystacks. Since almost no attention is paid in the story to the suitability of these partners, beyond (that is) their being available, the 'love' mentioned in the title might seem something of a misnomer. When Stendhal talks about love in *De l'amour* he concentrates on how baulked sexual desire leads to the idealisation of various features of the loved one and regards this process as far more important and valuable than the desire itself. There is no time for this in 'Love among the Haystacks' where both brothers are willing to take love for granted, and to commit their futures to almost any young women who can save them in their dire situation. In Schopenhauer's view, the forces that are driving them have no regard whatsoever for any question of future compatibility; but in Lawrence's, instinct is always to be trusted, as long as – and this is a teasing conundrum that will follow him throughout his life – it can be identified as genuine.

How sexual attraction relates to compatibility in other areas of life is nevertheless an issue which Lawrence does not entirely ignore. An early attempt to address it comes in the first version of an excellent novella eventually entitled *Daughters of the Vicar*. This tells the story of the two daughters of the Reverend Mr Lindley, the younger of whom is insistent that she should be physically attracted to the man she marries. Not finding much to her taste in her own social circle, she defiantly crosses the class barrier in order to attach herself to a young miner. The shock this causes Lindley and his wife demonstrates that their social snobbery is far stronger than their Christian charity. The girl's elder sister has previously accepted marriage with a visiting curate who has the sickly body of a boy of thirteen, but a healthy private income. Yet it is not so much the miner's lack of upper middle-class financial resources which distresses the vicar and his wife but his social status as an ordinary working man. 'I have my position to maintain, and a position which may not be taken lightly', the vicar says.[4] In the final version the young couple feel obliged to mollify him by saying they will emigrate to Canada, but in the one Lawrence finished in 1911 he attempted a description of Louisa and Alfred (as the two young people are called) in their married life, one main feature of which is Louisa's refusal or inability to associate with the other miners' wives. It must have been because he was dissatisfied with this that he ended *Daughters of the Vicar* with the callous insensitivity the vicar and his wife display when Alfred pays a visit to the vicarage in order to ask for their daughter's hand. This makes for a neat conclusion but could leave some readers wondering how two people whose educational and cultural backgrounds are so different would be able to make a life together. The conviction that they almost certainly wouldn't is Schopenhauerean in the sense that, for him, there is no reason to believe that natural impulses are present in human beings for their benefit rather than their eventual harm. But then this view is in tune with the settled pessimism which pervades all Schopenhauer's writings. At the very end of the 'Metaphysics of Love', for example, he refers to lovers who exchange secret glances as traitors to humankind because they are 'striving to perpetuate all this misery and turmoil that otherwise would come to a timely end'.[5] Lawrence would have none of this, even though the ideas of

Schopenhauer on love were ones he struggled to combat or qualify all his life.

LAWRENCE IN LOVE

Frieda Weekley was accustomed to leaving her husband and taking periodic trips back to Germany, where she had been born and brought up. Lawrence very soon accompanied her on one of these, as her secret lover. But the deception the two of them were then practising on Weekley troubled him, and he was uncomfortable with the way Frieda felt obliged to hide the nature of her relationship with him from certain members of her German family (in particular her father), so he insisted on writing a letter to Weekley which explained how things stood. 'I love your wife and she loves me' was one of the sentences in this letter.[6] They had gone to Germany in May 1912 and were there until September when they made their way to Gargnano on Lake Garda in Italy, where they stayed until April of the following year. The letters Lawrence wrote at this time are full of expressions of the love which follows rather than precedes consummation. In one of the earlier ones he sent to Frieda herself, for example, when she and Lawrence were temporarily separated, he said that 'Passion, that nearly drives one mad is far away from real love' and concluded, 'I shall love you all my life. That is also a new idea to me. But I believe it'. Later he wrote that he 'never knew what love was before' but that he and Frieda have 'struggled through some bad times into a wonderful naked intimacy that I know is love'. From Gargnano he wrote to say how wonderful it was to 'keep going further into love' and it was when he was there that he also made his famous remark about always being the priest of love.[7]

It is not difficult to find reasons for the effect Frieda had on Lawrence. As a young woman she was strikingly good-looking and though, when he first met her, she was six years older than he was, and the mother of three children, the photographs suggest she was still very attractive. She was in addition foreign with that appeal of the unusual to which Lawrence seems to have been responsive even before he met her (the woman who meets Maurice's needs in 'Love among the Haystacks' is the local vicar's German nanny), and which he attributes to Tom Brangwen. Frieda clearly had immediate sexual appeal for Lawrence and like his Maurice, or Louisa in *Daughters of the Vicar*, he was no doubt prepared to let issues of long-term compatibility look after themselves. For Louisa there is a class difference which is the reverse of the one Lawrence had to deal with in that Frieda was from a family of German aristocrats (the von Richthofens); but he had been educated to a stage where he knew how to act 'the gentleman', even if he rarely chose to do so, and intellectually he was her superior, as he would have been to most new acquaintances, male or female. Yet Frieda was no fool and had read things he hadn't. He was used to young women who were well-read and comfortable in discussion, but not to someone whose ideas were quite as avant-garde as hers were. One of several affairs she had had in the past was with Otto Gross, a disciple of Freud who caused the master some embarrassment when, as he began to practise psychoanalysis, he slept with some of his patients (he may have been the target, or one of the targets, of Freud's essay 'Wild Psychoanalysis'). Gross believed fervently in free love, a rare case of an expression in which sex is not merely to be assumed as part of love but could usually be substituted for it; and that all repression was wrong. It was her enthusiastic adoption of Gross's ideas which perhaps constituted Frieda's most immediate intellectual attraction for Lawrence, especially as it meant that, very quickly, and with very few social preliminaries, she was willing to have sex with him.

Lawrence fell in love with Frieda and the experience manifests itself from time to time in his later fiction, although much less so than in most other novelists who deal predominantly with the relations between the sexes; but did she love him as he claimed in his letter to Weekley that she did? And was it with an equal fervour? The several lovers she had had previously, both at home and abroad, had not destroyed her marriage; and as the mother of children she was not at first inclined to give up both them and her comfortable lifestyle for this most recent, impecunious one. But having found the most wonderful woman in all England, and seemingly resolved all his previous problems, Lawrence was looking for a relationship which was permanent. It was a tribute to his determination that he was eventually able to persuade her to abandon all she had in Nottingham and commit herself to him; and he could not have done that without strong feeling on her side. Following his death, she remembered how, shortly after their first meeting, she had gone with him on a walk with her children. When they came to a small brook

> Lawrence made the children some paper boats and put matches in them and let them float downstream under the bridge. Then he put daisies in the brook, and they floated downstream with their upturned faces. Crouched by the brook, playing there with the children, Lawrence forgot about me completely.
>
> Suddenly I knew I loved him. He had touched a new tenderness in me.[8]

This is a different kind of love from those one usually finds Lawrence dealing with in his early fiction, although very familiar from other writers (Madame Rênal's feeling for Julien in *Le rouge et le noir* has this same tender quality). It was reinforced in Frieda by the growing conviction that the young man who had accidentally come her way was a literary genius. Several of the women Lawrence had known before her were emancipated in the political sense. That is to say that, without necessarily being suffragettes themselves, they were sympathetic to the idea of more political power for women. But in the circles in which Frieda had moved in Germany, the ideal for a young woman was rather to discover a genius to whom she could act as an inspiration or muse. Gross had told her that she was 'the affirmation of [his] life, the flowering, fruitful yes' and a 'woman of the future'.[9] He had described how the new sexually liberated woman could be an inspiration for intellectual striving men (like himself presumably), but *a fortiori* for evidently gifted young artists such as Lawrence. This was a re-vamping of the old idea of woman as the handmaiden of genius but very different in nature and, in spite of all the major emotional and material sacrifices Frieda certainly made in order to stay with Lawrence, anyone who felt that pursuing this ideal meant any permanent practice of self-denial on her part, would not have known Frieda well.

FREUD

Lawrence's affair with Frieda, and his marriage to her in July 1914, had a profound effect on his writing (as she never tired of insisting). The early signs of this came in 1912 after Heinemann had rejected the penultimate version of *Sons and Lovers*, which was then called 'Paul Morel', for its 'want of reticence'.[10] As Lawrence set about a final revision under Frieda's influence, his view of the novel became increasingly 'Freudian'. The external indications of this are in the change of title but also the synopsis which Lawrence sent to Edward Garnett, the friend who had been able to find him an alternative publisher after Heinemann's rejection. There Lawrence says that as the sons in the Morel household grow up, their mother 'selects them as lovers' so that, when they come to manhood, 'they can't love, because their mother is the strongest power in their lives'. When the oldest boy 'gives his sex to a fribble', while his mother still 'holds his soul', 'the split kills him'. Paul's life follows a similar pattern but as 'the split begins to tell again', the mother almost unconsciously realises what is the matter and 'begins to die'.[11]

It is fortunate that the final changes Lawrence made to *Sons and Lovers* were not so radical that the novel ever became as crudely programmatic as his summary suggests: rather than giving his 'sex to a fribble', William Morel becomes engaged to a girl who is not a sensible person like his mother and then feels he has gone too far to extricate himself (a judgement that his mother supports), while it is hard on Mrs. Morel to suggest that her cancer is a matter of choice, even of unconscious choice. Yet the words in the summary do mark the beginning of a process which Frieda did much to initiate, and by which Lawrence's mother was increasingly held responsible for all her son's emotional difficulties. Of the very first occasion she and Lawrence were alone together, Frieda reports that they 'talked about Oedipus and understanding leaped through our words'; and when she read 'Paul Morel' for the first time she told Garnett that Lawrence had 'quite missed the point'. This was because, she explained, 'He really loved his mother more than any body … real love, sort of Oedipus'.[12] Blaming his mother for what he had become (a self-analysis she was no longer around to contest), meant also a gradual reversal of the harsh judgement Lawrence had been accustomed to pass on his father and provided him with an account of how children should *not* be brought up which he would later expound at some length.

When *Sons and Lovers* was first published, Ivy Low, the niece of one of England's first psychoanalysts, sent postcards to a number of her friends which read 'Discovered a genius! Be sure to read *Sons and Lovers*! This is a book about the Oedipus complex!'[13] With the knowledge she had derived of Freud from Otto Gross, Frieda had done much to produce this reaction although some of the moments in the novel which seem most obviously 'Freudian' cannot be ascribed with any certainty to her influence. After another family quarrel, for example, Paul is prompted to urge his mother not to sleep with his father ('Sleep with Annie, mother, not with him').[14] The source here could have been Freud but might just have credibly been the scene in *Hamlet* where the Prince gives his mother, also called Gertrude, similar advice. Always supposing, of course, that Lawrence needed such a source at all.

In the coming months and years, Lawrence gradually distanced himself from the version of Freud which he had imbibed, chiefly from Frieda. He seems to have at first welcomed her loosely Freudian talk as a possible way of enlarging his understanding of his own past, but was annoyed when the novel was seized on by committed admirers of Freud as an *exemplification* of Freudian theory. An account that especially irritated him appeared in *The Psychoanalytic Review* in 1916. 'My poor book', he complained, 'it was as art, a fairly complete truth; so they carve a half lie out of it and say "voilà". Swine!'.[15] It is not hard to see his point. Some of the finest scenes of *Sons and Lovers* are after all those in which first William and then Paul Morel are shown in sensitive and sometimes half-jocular communication with their mother. These have a tenderness and delicacy of dramatisation which make them particularly appealing: Mrs. Morel accompanying her son to Nottingham so that he can be interviewed for his first job would be a case in point. For a critic to insist that the details in these are of course manifestations of Oedipal feelings tends to be 'reductive' and harmful of their literary effect. When Lawrence told Compton Mackenzie that the only time he had known 'perfect love' during his adolescence was with another male, he was probably omitting to mention what he had felt for his mother because that was a phenomenon sufficiently familiar to be taken for granted. Yet whereas the bathing scene in *The White Peacock* clearly shows that there were sexual implications to that love of another man of which he was at the time unaware, there are no such suggestions, or at least very few, in what Lawrence writes about William or Paul with their mother. He would have been prepared for the Freudian approach by Schopenhauer's 'Every kind of love, however ethereal it may seem to be, springs entirely from the instinct of sex'; but there were large parts of *Sons and Lovers*, including the scenes I mention, that were already so well established that they appear to have been resistant to it.

By the time he complained about *The Psychoanalytic Review*, the greater knowledge of Freud's theories Lawrence possessed can be attributed not only to Frieda but also to his getting to know personally several of the leading English Freudians (including Ivy Low's aunt). What they said was eventually sufficiently challenging for him to produce, shortly after the First World War had ended, two short books on psychoanalysis and the unconscious. The second of these illustrates how relevant to Lawrence is Blake's dictum: 'I must create a system or be enslaved by another man's'; but in the first he makes some detailed criticisms of the Freudian position as he understood it, or as it was then understood. Since he identifies 'incest craving' as central to what Freud had to say, and since he assumes that repression is the main cause of all mental illness, he suggests that the Freudians are in the difficult position of having to tell their patients that they should sleep with their mothers or sisters in order to get well. In his view, however, the craving in question is a mind-generated phenomenon which tends to be pushed back into 'the sack of horrors' that is the Freudian unconscious, but does not belong to the most basic instinctual drives, those which reside in an unconscious Lawrence calls 'pristine'.[16] What makes Lawrence a Romantic is that he believes, with Rousseau, that these can never be unpleasant or at fault. In that context, of course, Freud could by contrast be called a follower of Hobbes, as could Schopenhauer.

Incest craving in Freud is associated with *infantile* sexuality, one of the most distinctive aspects of his thinking. That many men have possessive mothers, and tend to resent their fathers when they are growing up, is after all hardly news, and only in a very loose sense amounts to what is called the Oedipus complex. That necessitates sexual feelings between mothers and the very young child which some adults fail to work through satisfactorily. Lawrence's criticism is the same as Jung's and consists in claiming that if people are able to dredge up memories from early childhood which have a strong sexual content, it is because they have invested them with sexuality *retrospectively*. Like Freud – and like Schopenhauer – Lawrence often wrote as if he believed that sex was primary; and he accepted Otto Gross's view that all repression was evil (his mother's cancer he tended more and more to think of as one of its consequences, rather than a method she had unconsciously chosen to free her son from her influence). But he could take up this latter position with relative ease because he believed there was nothing in the 'pristine unconscious', and could be nothing, that should or needed to be repressed.

While acknowledging how intensely he had loved his mother, and occasionally suggesting that there was something abnormal in his attachment to her, Lawrence does not seem to have been entirely convinced that he had ever had feelings for her which could properly be described as sexual. In *Fantasia of the Unconscious* (1921), the second of the two books I refer to, he made a determined effort to *argue* the case against Freud. He establishes there what he calls a 'biological psyche', with nerve centres – or in the word he had borrowed from a book on yoga that had had a powerful influence on him, 'chakras' – at the back of the body which allow the individual to develop independence, pride and separation from the world; and an equivalent, corresponding number at the front which are outgoing and sympathetic. It is the crime of mothers like his own to over-stimulate the latter at the expense of the former, so that a child becomes sensitive, loving and intuitive but insufficiently robust, too inclined to absorb itself into what is Other rather than standing apart. However,

> Our psyche is so framed that activity aroused on one plane provokes activity on the corresponding plane, automatically. So the intense *pure* love-relation between parent and child inevitably arouses the lower centres in the child, the centres of sex. Now the deeper sensual centres, once aroused, should find response from the sensual body of some other, some friend or lover. The response is impossible between parent and child. Myself, I believe that biologically there is a radical sex-aversion between parent and child, at the

deeper sensual centres. The sensual circuit *cannot* adjust itself spontaneously between the two.[17]

Although the manner here is ratiocinative, there is in it more assertion than argument. It does not help that the biology to which Lawrence constantly appeals is used in a way which is bogus (not that pseudo-science is not sometimes characteristic of Freud also).

Fantasia was a long way in the future when Lawrence and Frieda began living together and it has to be said that earlier there had been good reasons why she should have felt Freud's thinking was applicable to him. A poem Lawrence wrote before they met, for example, is called 'Hymn to Priapus' and begins:

> My love lies underground
> With her face upturned to mine,
> And her mouth unclosed in a last long kiss
> That ended her life and mine.

It is not every young man who would write about his dead mother in this way. The poem goes on to describe how he has been to a Christmas party (his mother died in early December) and been intimate in some way which is not made specific with a 'big, soft country lass'. He feels that this is a betrayal of his mother, and not simply because he should be in mourning. The only remedy, he concludes, is to be 'faithless and faithful' together.[18] There is a tinge of strange eroticism in most of the poems he writes about his mother at this time, and later. Two that deal with her when she was either dying or already dead would eventually be entitled 'The Bride' and 'The Virgin Mother'. They focus on the fact that when all the pain and stress of dying is past, the dead can seem surprisingly youthful. Sometime in the first two years of her relationship with Lawrence, Frieda found in his notebooks a draft of what would become 'The Virgin Mother', the second stanza of which reads:

> My little love, my dearest,
> Twice you have borne me,
> Once from your womb, sweet mother,
> Once from myself, to be
> Free of all hearts of people,
> Of each heart's home-life free.[19]

Frieda would have disputed the second claim made here but the poem went on to declare, of his mother, 'I shall always be true to thee'. She scribbled all over it her intense dislike of the sentiments it expressed and, after accusing its author of freely choosing to commit himself to 'a sad, old woman's misery', commented that she had nearly killed herself 'in the battle to get you in connection with myself and other people, sadly I proved to myself that *I* can love, but *never* you'.[20] What the draft ('My Love, My Mother') appears to have shown her is that Lawrence's mother continued to dominate his feelings after her death and was a major impediment to her establishing a proper relation with him. That she should have found what Gross had told her about Freud relevant to Lawrence's situation is not therefore surprising, however rudimentary her application of Freudian theory might have been. Because it had been in gestation for so long, and contained so many layers, *Sons and Lovers* was resilient to having too much of a Freudian pattern imposed upon it; but the poems about his dead mother are a different matter. Far more directly autobiographical, they already show a tendency to sexualise the love Lawrence had felt for her, in spite of the 'radical sex-aversion' between parent and child he was later to refer to in *Fantasia* and if only, to echo Jung's criticism of Freud, retrospectively. The difficult and perhaps insoluble question they raise is that whether they show Lawrence to have always been a suitable case for psychoanalytic treatment or a writer apt, at certain moments of his career, to seize on a particular vocabulary and intellectual framework because he found it convenient. To employ his own distinction, it is hard to know whether whatever eroticism there is in them is mind-generated or pristine.[21]

TESTING TIMES

Just how far instinct can be trusted, and whether people who are drawn together sexually have enough in common in other ways to live together amicably, were questions Lawrence was now in a position to answer from personal experience. It will be evident from what Frieda had to say about his relationship to his mother that, even in its early phase, life was far from peaceful. Because Lawrence had very quickly become as fervent a believer in the evils of repression as his future wife, they often expressed their feelings as and when they occurred, and began that habit of quarrelling violently in public which so startled their friends once they were back in England. It was a way they had of clearing the air but that their problems were deep and long-standing is evident from a patently autobiographical short story Lawrence wrote only a year after he and Frieda had been together.

Called 'New Eve and Old Adam', this deals with a man called Peter Moest and his wife Paula and the action begins when a telegram is delivered to their flat which reads 'Meet me Marble Arch 7.30 – theatre – Richard'.[22] It will turn out that the telegram has been delivered to the wrong address but, because her husband's jealousy has been excited, Paula conceals the fact that she has no idea who Richard is. There is little room for male jealousy in her scheme of things, as there wasn't in Frieda's. How could there be when all repression, especially repression of sexual desire, was wrong; and Frieda had not left Weekley in order to be hamstrung by old notions of marital fidelity (although in fact she had not found them too difficult to evade previously). When she and Lawrence were walking over the mountains from southern Germany into Italy in April 1912, and were accompanied for a while by Edward Garnett's son, David, and his friend Harold Hobson (both in their early twenties), she became irritated with Lawrence and abruptly informed him that she had had sex with Hobson a few days previously.[23] In her view, their relationship and later marriage would always be what is now called 'open', open for both although she knew very well that Lawrence's temperament and upbringing made infidelity very difficult for him. In 'New Eve and Old Adam' Moest has just returned from Paris and Paula mocks the idea that, even though they have been seriously at odds with each other, he could have seized the opportunity for extra-marital sex – 'You and Parisian Nights' Entertainment! What a fool you would look',[24] just as she mocks (or tests) him by concealing that she knows no-one called Richard.

As the story continues, the complaints each have of the other begin to be expressed. Moest is convinced that 'physically … [Paula] loved him, or had loved him, and was satisfied, or had been satisfied'. Yet, just like Clara Dawes, she feels that when they make love her husband often seems to be obeying 'some impersonal instinct for which she was the only outlet'; although she adds a new dimension to Clara's charge by claiming that 'sometimes she thought he was a big fountain pen which was always sucking her blood for ink'. In her view, by using her to reach regions where individuality does not matter, or by valuing only the experiences she can offer (and he can write about) rather than what she is 'in herself', he shows himself incapable of real love. At several points in the story, she caresses and arouses him, and calls on him to say he loves her. But experience has taught Moest to be suspicious and he accuses Paula of having treated him 'like a piece of cake, for you to eat when you wanted'.

The strength of Paula's feelings for Moest means that her love can quickly turn to hate. When he decides not to stay in the flat but instead spend the night in a nearby hotel, after Paula has given him the impression she will not be prevented from meeting the mysterious Richard, he discovers that, 'Since she had begun to hate him, he had gradually lost that physical pride and pleasure in his own physique which the first months of married life had given him. His body had gone meaningless to him again, almost as if it were not there.' He spends a very uncomfortable night, thinking of 'Richard' although less because of whom he might be and more because he recognises him as a means Paula is using to fight free of the 'close, basic intimacy in which she had been drawn' with her husband, and which he so much values. A sign of the need and dependency which humiliates him is that he sends Paula a note from the hotel to tell her where he is staying, and there is both relief and resistance when, in the morning, he receives back a telegram from her which reads, 'Come to tea, my dear love'. More than anything he needs the relationship to be preserved, but is not sure he wants to be her 'dear love'.

When Moest arrives back at the flat for tea, he finds his wife is already entertaining a young man. It turns out he is also called Moest, is living in the same block of flats and has a cousin called Richard. This resolution of the puzzle of the telegram relieves Moest of one anxiety but he develops another as he notices how interested his wife is in the visitor, a young poet who 'had never been in touch with life save through literature'. When he leaves and they discuss him, Paula describes it as a crime that the young man should be stuck up among his literary gods, like a minor ornament on the mantelpiece 'while all his youth is gone'. When Moest says that he ought to learn to climb down from the mantelpiece himself, she responds tartly with 'Did *you* get off your miserable starved isolation by yourself? – you didn't. You had to be fetched down, and I had to do it'. He can see she is tempted to adopt this other, younger Moest as 'her mission', just as she had him a year ago: 'There was no core to the woman. She was full of generosity and bigness and kindness, but there was no heart in her, no security, no place for one single man'. Once more they are seriously at odds and he talks of going to spend some time in Italy and decides that he will not be staying to dinner. But then Paula again makes a physical approach: '"My love", she said, in a little singing, abstract fashion, her lips

somehow sipping towards him, her eyes shining dilated'. Although
he feels 'as if he were not in it, himself', he cannot resist her since
for him the connection with Paula is 'bigger than life or death'. At
dinner, she makes much of him but without his ever quite feeling
like the lord she treats him as being, but rather one of the dolls to
which she must as a child have pretended to subject herself, no
more (that is) than her 'lordliest plaything'. When they begin to
kiss and she asks once again whether he loves her, he can only answer, with a struggle, 'you know': 'he loved to be made much of by
her. But he had a dim, hurting sense that she would not love him
tomorrow'. Thus although the couple is reconciled, it is no surprise
to learn, at the very end of 'New Eve and Old Adam', that Moest
has indeed gone to Italy. When Paula writes to him there, she says
that he has undermined her 'in some subtle, corrupt way' by pre-
tending to love her when he does not know what love is.[25]

Moest is confident that, physically speaking, Paula was satisfied by him, or *had been*. Despite this ominous qualification,
'New Eve and Old Adam' is much less about sex than love and
represents the beginning of a searching examination of how feelings which may appear self-sacrificing, can be a cover for various
forms of egotism. It is a commentary on Lawrence's relationship
with Frieda which he also continued in his poetry. In 1917 he
brought together many of the poems that dealt with that relationship and published them under the title of *Look! We Have Come
Through!* This strikes an optimistic note belied by the 'Argument'
which he seems to have composed shortly before publication and
which runs as follows:

> After much struggling and loss in love and in the world of
> man, the protagonist throws in his lot with a woman who
> is already married. Together they go into another country,
> she perforce leaving her children behind. The conflict of
> love and hate goes on between the man and the woman,

and between these two and the world around them, till it reaches some sort of conclusion.[26]

The reference here to 'hate', and the final four words, give a more accurate impression of the poems which follow than the triumphalism in the collection's title. Not free of a certain retrospective rationalisation, the poems are somewhat thrown together, like many of those in Lawrence's collections before 1928, and by no means all of them are relevant to what purports to be the controlling narrative. Some do not have much literary merit but only become interesting when they are related to biographical details of Lawrence and Frieda's life together. They can then become very interesting, chiefly because the extent to which Lawrence is willing, in poems which are explicitly autobiographical, to display to a general public details of his most intimate experiences remains astonishing. But an example of where biographical interest and literary merit may well coincide is the poem in *Look!* called '"She said as well to me."' Written much later than 'New Eve and Old Adam', it elaborates on that not very felicitous moment in the story when Moest accuses Paula of treating him like 'a piece of cake'.[27] In the first part of the poem a woman is asking a man not to be ashamed of his naked body: 'Straight and clean is the body of a man, / such an instrument, a spade, or an oar, / such a joy to me –'. Feeling that he is 'a tool in the hand of the Lord' that only God could have shaped, she presses her hands down his sides so that he begins to wonder over himself: 'I admire you so, you are beautiful: this clean sweep of your sides, this firmness, this hard mould'. She is reminded of how, as a child, she used to love to handle her father's riding whip ('it seemed like a near part of him'), and his pens. This appreciation is what Moest regrets being deprived of in those periods when Paula hates him but the effect in the poem is quite different as the man responds to the woman's eulogy of his body:

> Now I say to her: 'No tool, no instrument, no God!
> Don't touch me and appreciate me.
> It is an infamy.
> You would think twice before you touched a weasel on a
>   fence
> as it lifts its straight white throat.
> Your hand would not be so flig and easy.[28]

He wonders in conclusion why there seems to her nothing in him which should make her hesitate, and feels that there is in fact plenty, if she would only recognise it. This throws an interesting light on those moments in 'New Eve and Old Adam' when Moest is never quite comfortable when Paula takes the physical initiative and begins to make love to him. He has enjoyed being made much of, and his wife's appreciation of him has transformed his life and is now something he feels he cannot do without; yet at the same time (in what is a mirror image of feelings both Paula and Clara Dawes experience) he has a lurking suspicion of being used and dominated. This is a paradox from which Lawrence himself would never be free.

WILL AND ANNA

Paula Moest claims to have saved her husband and made (or tried to make) a man of him. Frieda would have said the same and Lawrence would not have denied it. In the early days of their relationship, he not only credited her with allowing him to escape his solipsism but also frequently insisted that the quite new kind of writing he was able to do came from both of them. There was the final version of *Sons and Lovers* but after that *The Sisters*, the eventual source of both *The Rainbow* and *Women in Love*, two of the most original novels English Literature had yet seen. In these, it was not a question of more or less autobiographical transcription, but of a fully imagined creation emanating from the different, far more experienced person Frieda had helped Lawrence to become.

children

When in *The Rainbow* Tom Brangwen eventually marries Lydia
Lensky, he acquires not only a wife but also a step-daughter called
Anna. The account of his relations with Anna, who is still a child, is
one of the strongest parts of the novel but then it is hard to think of
anyone who describes children better than Lawrence. That might
at first seem surprising given that he had no children himself. There
were, however, plenty of them in his immediate environment, although that could not have helped him to recount so effectively
and movingly Tom's feelings when Anna is about to get married,
and he realises he is on the point of losing her. That success has to
be put down to the ability of great writers to send their imagination
into areas where they have never been themselves.

Anna's future husband is her cousin Will Brangwen and there
is no *coup de foudre* to initiate their relationship. That builds up
slowly until their marriage after which, in one of the most powerful parts of this or any other novel, Lawrence sets out to track
closely how their feelings for each other develop. Fully imagined
though this is, it is impossible to imagine him fulfilling that task
in the particular way he does without his having first met Frieda.
There is initially the period of the honeymoon, when both are
in a sensual trance, staying in bed most of the day and ignoring
completely the workaday world, and when Anna teaches Will to
accept his own and her nakedness and lose his inhibitions. Only
when that is over do both begin the struggle to come to terms
with living in such close and intimate proximity with another human being. For each one of them there are times when not to be
on one's own, to 'have one's space' as people say nowadays, can be
intolerable. 'He came in to the house. The sound of his footsteps
in his heavy boots filled her with horror: a hard, cruel, malignant
sound', thinks Anna at one moment; but later she retaliates by
turning in the evening to her sewing, in a way she knows he de-
tests: 'He hated beyond measure to hear the shriek of the calico
as she tore the web sharply, as if with pleasure. And the run of the
sewing-machine gathered a frenzy in him at last'.[29] These are only

superficial indications of an oscillation between love and hate (to echo the terms of *Look!*'s 'Argument') which can be violent in the extreme, in part because the love has been so strong:

> There followed two black and ghastly days, when she was set in anguish against him, and he felt as if he were in a black and violent underworld, and his wrists quivered murderously. And she resisted him. He seemed a dark, almost evil thing pursuing her, hanging on to her, burdening her. She would give anything to have him removed.[30]

There is both dialogue and dramatisation in Lawrence's account, introduced with his usual deft economy, especially in those parts where Anna goes back home to seek temporary refuge with her parents, or is protesting against Will's mystical, non-analytic absorption in religious images (which she dimly perceives as a threat to their relationship); but its main emphasis lies on conveying the feelings which lie just below the surface of consciousness, belonging as they to do to two people who may be more articulate than Tom Brangwen, but are only marginally so. At this stage in his career, and bearing always in mind what he must have felt it was possible to publish, when Lawrence wants to indicate how the conflicts Will and Anna experience are reflected in their sexual encounters – if they are not sometimes also precipitated by them – he can usually only do so via metaphor:

> And she loved the intent, far look of his eyes when they rested on her: intent, yet far, not near, not with her. And she wanted to bring them nearer. She wanted his eyes to come to hers, to know her. And they would not. They remained intent, and far, and proud, like a hawk's, naïve and inhuman as a hawk's. So she loved him and caressed him and roused him like a hawk, till he was keen and instant, but without tenderness. He came to her fierce and hard,

like a hawk striking and taking her. He was no mystic any more, she was his aim and object, his prey. And she was carried off, and he was satisfied, or satiated at last.

Then immediately she began to retaliate on him. ...[31]

This is recognisably Anna and Will having sex, but seen at a distance and with an absence of sharp detail. To Will's distress, Anna begins to feel oppressed by the closeness of her partner in bed, accuses him of exerting his malign will against her, and demands that they should sleep apart.

This particular crisis comes when Anna is pregnant. Knowing she is going to have a child gives her life an orientation which, to his dismay and anger, tends to reduce Will to a minor role. In the scene where, naked and in the later stages of her pregnancy, she celebrates her own fertility with eurhythmic movements, Anna is described by Lawrence as effecting Will's 'nullification' and 'non-existence' in her dance.[32] With at this stage no creative outlet of his own, having abandoned the religious carving with which he had previously been struggling, and no interest in his work, he is much more dependent on Anna than she is now on him, and in any emotional power struggle (which is what their marriage has quickly become), the weaker partner is always the one with the most need. The self-sufficiency Anna develops only increases after the birth of her child and is one of the factors driving Will to seek temporary sexual satisfaction outside the house; but after he has failed to seduce a 'little creature in Nottingham', his wife recognises something different about him as soon as he comes home, as if he were absolved from his usual 'humble, good self'. Instead of being angry, she instinctively decides to play him at his own game: 'she too was out for her own adventure'. That is to say 'she too could throw everything overboard, love, intimacy, responsibility', and make their relationship a matter of 'seeking gratification pure and simple'. Their sexual life therefore becomes one where each is wholly focussed on deriving as much personal

pleasure as possible from the other: 'there was no tenderness, no
love between them any more, only the maddening, sensuous lust
for discovery'.[33] Sexual experimentation, varieties of love-making
or what some would call perversity, seems a logical progression
from this state of affairs. Boldly explicit as Lawrence is about this
general transformation in Will and Anna's relationship, he is understandably less so when it comes to details:

> But still the thing terrified [Will]. Awful and threatening
> it was, dangerous to a degree, even whilst he gave himself
> to it. It was pure darkness, also. All the shameful things
> of the body revealed themselves to him now with a sort
> of sinister, tropical beauty. All the shameful, natural and
> unnatural acts of sensual voluptuousness which he and
> the woman partook of together, created together, they had
> their heavy beauty and delight. Shame, what was it? It was
> part of extreme delight. It was that part of which man is
> usually afraid. Why afraid? The secret, shameful things are
> most terribly beautiful.
>
> They accepted shame, and were at one with it in their
> most unlicensed pleasures. It was incorporated. It was a
> bud that blossomed into beauty and heavy, fundamental
> gratification.[34]

It is usually assumed that when *The Rainbow* was banned, it was
because of a lesbian episode involving Anna's daughter Ursula and
her school teacher, as well perhaps on account of a good deal of
anti-war rhetoric in Ursula's dialogue. Passages like the one above
were no doubt too obscure to attract attention. Whatever the specific practices to which it alludes, only a puritanical consciousness
like Will's, or like that of Lawrence himself, could surround them
with so much mystery and melodrama. Yet episodes in later books
make it as clear as these things can be that 'fundamental gratification' is Lawrentian code for anal intercourse.

Anal intercourse between heterosexuals will become a recurrent theme in Lawrence's writing from this time on (as early as 1914 Middleton Murry reported that, in one of their violent public quarrels, Frieda complained that her husband had the habit of taking her 'as a dog does a bitch', a remark which could mean several things but in context probably only means one).[35] Quite what the general significance of this practice should be – how it should be interpreted – is difficult to say given that the fictional contexts in which it occurs vary a good deal. Here it chiefly indicates that Will and Anna have reached a stage where they are using each other's bodies for personal satisfaction, largely (that is) for sex without love or tenderness. Where that eventually leads is a question readers might reasonably begin to ask, but it is one Lawrence does not choose to answer since he fairly quickly switches the focus in *The Rainbow* away from Will and Anna and on to their daughter Ursula. When they reappear in *Women in Love* they have become a dull, conventional couple and there is a cruel moment in that novel when Ursula and her younger sister Gudrun have momentarily returned to the house which the other members of their family have just vacated. They sit together in their parents' now empty bedroom and ponder what Will and Anna's marriage has meant. 'It all seems so *nothing*, their two lives', Ursula says, '– there's no meaning in it. Really, if they had *not* met, and *not* married, and not lived together – it wouldn't have mattered, would it?'[36]

HOMOSEXUALITY

The anal intercourse between heterosexuals which begins to figure quite frequently in Lawrence's writing after *The Rainbow* has been interpreted by some commentators as a further sign of repressed homosexuality, a fact which would come as a surprise to those heterosexuals who make it part of their own love-making, and certainly to large sections of the porn industry. It can tell both for and against this claim that, in one of his most successful short stories, Lawrence exhibits a quite exceptional inwardness with how homosexual desire can be diverted and repressed. He was never of course in the army himself, but Frieda came from a military family and he seems to have imbibed from her an understanding of the military as an obvious place for the development of homoerotic relations, and on occasions something more. 'The Prussian Officer' was written in 1913 and deals with the attraction the officer of the title begins to experience for one of the young soldiers he commands. Since all his training prevents him from expressing this in a straightforward manner, his feelings prompt him to a sadistic persecution of the soldier (who has a girlfriend at home). This becomes so extreme that the soldier kills the officer, and destroys his own future in the process. The power with which this sad and terrible tale is unfolded is so remarkable that some might feel its author must have been able to identify and deal with his own repressions or (in the case of anal intercourse) displacements. But for others that is made unlikely by the understanding the story displays seeming so much more intuitive than conceptual.[37]

The naivety about homosexuality Lawrence manifests in *The White Peacock* soon evaporated and it became a topic to which he gave a good deal of serious thought. Henry Savage was a writer whom Lawrence met in 1913 when he and Frieda were briefly back in England. He had been a friend of the poet Richard Middleton, who had committed suicide in 1911, and Savage sent examples of this dead friend's work to the Lawrences once they were back in Italy (in Fiascherino, on the Gulf of Spezia, rather than on Lake Garda). It was from there Lawrence told Savage that he had concluded from reading Middleton that 'he would have loved a man, more than a woman: even physically'. 'I should like to know', he went on, 'why nearly every man that approaches greatness tends to homosexuality, whether he admits it or not: so that he loves the *body* of a man better than the body of a woman'. The trouble is, in Lawrence's view, that this love is a projection of a man's own image on to another male, as in a mirror, whereas, if he goes to a woman, it is to be 're-born, reconstructed. …but it is the hardest thing in life to get ones soul and body satisfied from a woman, so that one is free from oneself. And one is kept by all tradition and instinct from loving men, or a man'.[38]

Lawrence's words to Savage are the beginnings of an analysis he would develop and refine as time went on. At the centre of it is the idea that one man's body is too much like that of another to avoid self-enclosure, and that it is only by meeting the challenge of difference, which a woman's body (and nature) represents, that men can free themselves from solipsism. It was in March 1915, after the outbreak of the First World War had more or less trapped them in England and they were living in Sussex, that the Lawrences received that visit from E. M. Forster already mentioned. On the day he left, Lawrence wrote a long letter to Bertrand Russell in part of which he puzzles over Forster's case. As an introduction to the relevant passages, he asks why he himself goes to a woman. The answer this time is not so much to free as to know himself: 'What do I then embrace her for, hold the unknown against me? To repeat the experience of self-discovery.' If (that is) he has already discovered himself, he is then only repeating an already known reaction upon himself and indulging in what he calls 'sensationalism'. This is an awkward corollary of one of the meanings Lawrence wanted to place on sexual intercourse in heterosexual relations: if it allowed the man to free or discover himself, it has no more useful function after that aim had been achieved. But he ignores this problem and, in a dubious shift, quickly moves on to suggesting that when men begin repeating known reactions on themselves, 'there is always Sodomy':

> The man goes to the man to repeat this reaction upon himself. It is a nearer form of masterbation (sic). But still it has some *object* – there are still two bodies instead of one. A man of strong soul has too much honour for the other

body – man or woman – to use it as a means of masterba-
tion. So he remains neutral, inactive. That is Forster.[39]

The logic of these remarks would suggest that, at this stage at least, Lawrence was largely or might just as well have been neutral and inactive also.

It was Lady Ottoline Morrell who had enabled Lawrence to get to know Russell quite well. Her country house in Garsington was a meeting place for numerous artists and thinkers, united for the most part in their opposition to the war. Among the visitors was Lytton Strachey, and other members of what is now called Bloomsbury for whom homosexuality was either a way of life or easily accepted. In March 1915, shortly after Forster's visit, Russell invited Lawrence to spend a weekend with him in Cambridge where he was introduced to another prominent member of the Bloomsbury group in Maynard Keynes. There are all kinds of reasons of class and educational background which might have made this an uncomfortable visit for Lawrence – it would have been hard for Russell to avoid displaying him as some kind of grown-up, working-class *Wunderkind* – but there is not too much evidence of discomfort until about three weeks later when he wrote to David Garnett who had just visited the Lawrences along with his friend Francis Birrell. There is then a delayed reaction to the Cambridge experience which can only be described as hysterical:

> I can't bear to think of you, David, so wretched as you
> are … It is foolish of you to say that it doesn't matter ei-
> ther way – the men loving men. It doesn't matter in the
> public way. But it matters so much, David, to the man
> himself … that it is like a blow of triumphant decay, when
> I meet Birrell or the others. I simply can't bear it. It is so
> wrong, it is unbearable. It takes a form of inward corrup-
> tion which truly makes me scarce able to live. Why is there
> this horrible sense of frowstiness, so repulsive, as if it came

from deep inward dirt – a sort of sewer – deep in men like
K[eynes] and B[irrell] and D[uncan] G[rant]. It is something almost unbearable to me.[40]

Lawrence goes on to explain that it is not a question of moral disapproval and that he never considered Plato or Oscar Wilde wrong;
but that he did not really know what homosexuality was until he
saw Keynes emerging from the bedroom of the set of rooms where
he and Russell had gone to visit him at noon, standing there in his
pyjamas and blinking from sleep. The knowledge that had passed
into him then, Lawrence says, had been like 'a little madness' ever
since: 'And it was carried along with the most dreadful sense of re-
pulsiveness – something like carrion –a vulture gives me the same
feeling. I begin to feel mad as I think of it – insane'. Lawrence then
insists that he never wants to see Birrell again, that there is something nasty about him which makes him think of black beetles:

> He is horrible and unclean. I feel as if I should go mad, if I
> think of your set, D.G. and K. and B. It makes me dream
> of beetles. In Cambridge I had a similar dream. Somehow,
> I can't bear it. It is wrong beyond all bounds of wrongness.
> I had felt it slightly before, in the Stracheys. But it came full
> upon me in K., and in D.G. And yesterday I had it again,
> in B.'

He urges Garnett to leave 'these "friends", these beetles' and grow
whole by loving a woman, giving up 'this blasphemy against love'.
He himself, he repeats, did not know homosexuality was wrong
until he saw 'K. that morning in Cambridge': it was one of the cri-
ses of his life and sent him mad with 'misery, hostility and rage'.[41]

This is an untypical outburst of homophobic anger not easy to
explain: very shortly afterwards Lawrence would be taking a much
calmer approach to practising homosexuals, and in his later life
many of them were his friends. The puzzle is why it should have

been provoked by the sight of Keynes blinking in his pyjamas. It could be that Lawrence was living through what is known in Freudian circles as a 'reaction formation' to his own homosexual desires, or that Keynes suddenly became the focus of a number of other and quite different anxieties Lawrence was experiencing in Cambridge. Yet it could be also that the most important person in the whole picture was David Garnett, or 'Bunny' as he was affectionately known. Both Lawrence and Frieda were very fond of Garnett, and admirers of his physique; and the fact that he was accompanied on his visit to them by Francis Birrell, who was in love with him and may have been more overtly homosexual than they found comfortable, could have been influential. It may even be that it was only at this stage that Lawrence realised Bunny was bisexual and the lover of Duncan Grant. Whatever the reasons, it is characteristic that the disturbance which the confrontation with homosexuality in Cambridge, and perhaps afterwards, provoked in Lawrence should express itself in advice to others as to how they should live their lives, a phenomenon which Garnett resented (as Forster had before him). Entering Lawrence's vocabulary for the first time in relation to Garnett, however, is the association of homosexuality with a sewer. What will become clear later is that this is because it involves anal intercourse and the anus is the source, more obviously than the vagina or the female genitalia in general, of waste matter.

Women in Love and its 'Prologue'

Not long after the banning of *The Rainbow* in November 1915, Lawrence and Frieda retreated to Cornwall, as far away from the war as they could get. Their relationship since they had been forced to stay in England had been a troubled one, with at least one period of deliberate separation, but then the external pressures on them were considerable. The banning of *The Rainbow* made it difficult for Lawrence to publish and threatened him with dire poverty; Weekley had been successful in taking legal action which prevented Frieda from seeing her children; and she found herself among people who were at war with her home country (Manfred von Richthofen, the 'red baron', who was Germany's best known fighter pilot, was also her cousin). But there were other problems, more intimately related to their living and sleeping together, which made life difficult.

'The Sisters', that novel which Lawrence had begun in his first months of being with Frieda, had opened with Ursula and Gudrun Brangwen already young women, so that it was only in working back to give them some background that the material which was to go into *The Rainbow* was written. In Cornwall, Lawrence decided to look again at the continuation of Ursula's story (in the novel which became *Women in Love*) even though he must have felt, after what had happened to its predecessor, that the prospects for publication were very poor. In April 1916, a few months after his arrival in Cornwall, he wrote what is known as a 'Prologue' to the novel. This astonishing document was never published but is nonetheless a lion in the path for anyone trying to think about Lawrence, love and sex. It describes how Rupert Birkin, who has been a fellow of an Oxford college and is now a school inspector, is in the last stages of a relationship with Herm-ione Roddice. She worships his mind but seems to feel that the sexual contacts she has with him are only a necessary and not entirely welcome corollary of being able to keep his company, and gives her body to him in a spirit of self-sacrifice. This leaves Birkin so dissatisfied that he periodically goes off to have sex with women who are less 'spiritual', and even occasionally with pros-titutes. At the same time, he is subterraneanously aware of his growing attraction to a mutual friend of both himself and Herm-ione, Gerald Crich. Birkin comes to realise that 'although he was always drawn to women, feeling more at home with women than with a man, yet it was for men he felt the hot, flushing, roused attraction which a man is supposed to feel for the other sex'; that 'the male physique had a fascination for him; and for the female physique he felt only a fondness, a sort of sacred love, as for a sister'. He finds himself aroused by observing good-looking young men in the street, or sitting next to a young soldier in the train: 'In his mind was a small gallery of such men, men whom he had never spoken to, but who had flashed themselves upon his senses unforgettably, men whom he apprehended intoxicatingly in his blood'. Whenever, on the other hand, Birkin has been in contact with a woman, 'there entered in too much spiritual, sisterly love; or else, in reaction, there was only a brutal, callous sort of lust'. He is anxious to suppress his attraction to men, which is described as only spasmodic ('for weeks it would all be gone from him'), but 'what is suppression but a mere negation of life, and of living'. What he does do, however, is keep the secret 'even from himself. He knew what he felt, but he always kept the knowledge at bay'.[42]

Perhaps the first point to make about the 'Prologue' is how it illustrates the pitfalls of biographical reading. The Hermione Roddice mentioned in it already has some of the physical characteristics and social background which that character would possess in the final, published version of *Women in Love*, and which so upset Lady Ottoline Morrell. She must have felt that to be so recognisably and unflatteringly depicted was a poor return for the hospitality she had offered Lawrence at Garsington. All of their common friends concluded that, to all intents and purposes, the model for Hermione had indeed been Lady Ottoline; and yet as far as any supposed *sexual* relation between Hermione and Birkin is concerned, it is demonstrable that Lawrence was relying not on anything of that nature which had occurred between him and Lady Ottoline, since nothing had, but on his memories of his long association with Jessie Chambers. Jessie recognised this as soon as she was able to read *Women in Love* and had she seen the 'Prologue' she might well have felt that it gave a fairer assessment of her relation with Lawrence than 'The Test on Miriam', if only because, in the later, more disguised account, much of the blame for the failure is shifted to the male. What is striking is how closely its analysis of what troubles Birkin corresponds to the scenario Freud had sketched out in his 1910 essay about the 'Universal Tendency to Debasement in the Sphere of Love'. Whether that could be attributed to what Lawrence had learnt about Freud by 1916, or the reality of the situation they both describe, would be impossible to say.

Yet making clear that Hermione is in certain instances based on Jessie Chambers rather than Ottoline Morrell: that she is, like so many other characters in his fiction, a creative amalgam of people he had known, would be an unconvincing way of escaping the question of whether the experiences attributed to Birkin in the 'Prologue' were Lawrence's own. If they were (and it seems very likely), they clearly relate to that earlier period of his life when he was close to Jessie but not sexually attracted to her, and the idea may have been to show, in the coming novel, how Birkin was rescued from his preference for male bodies by Ursula, a woman for whom he *can* feel sexual attraction without her having to be degraded. That is only implicitly dramatised in the published version of *Women in Love* where Birkin is nevertheless shown strongly attracted to Gerald Crich in what he feels constitutes a necessary addition to his relation with Ursula, but she regards as a perversity. When he persuades Gerald that they should take off all their clothes and wrestle in the nude, it is perhaps the closest Lawrence ever came in fiction to making homoerotic attraction fully physical, and perhaps the closest he could come in writing which he still retained some hope of presenting to the public.

The obvious difference between the bathing scene in *The White Peacock* and the naked wrestling in *Women in Love* is the degree of self-understanding the author demonstrates. In the 'Prologue', Birkin is described as keeping the secret of his attraction to men from himself: 'he knew what he felt but always kept the knowledge at bay';[43] but his creator is aware of what is involved in a way he was not in his first novel. Meeting Keynes in Cambridge had given

Lawrence a lot to think about and homosexuality is a theme which occurs regularly in the speculative or philosophical writing which he appears to have been forced into writing by the distress of living in an England more and more dominated by the First World War. *The Signature* was a journal he and his close friend Middleton Murry conceived as a protest against the war. Lawrence called his contribution 'The Crown' and in a later section, which the collapse of *The Signature* left unpublished, he elaborated on an idea that would prove very important for *Women in Love*. This was that there were periods like the current one when whole communities could be involved in what he called a river or 'flux of dissolution'. At those times homosexuality becomes an 'inevitable part of the activity of reduction, of the flux of dissolution'. If homosexuals are attracted to men who are 'to a certain degree less developed than themselves', it is because they have a basic desire to get back to a state which has long been surpassed. The process of reduction and dissolution, that is, is also one of regression.[44]

'The Crown' was written before Lawrence went to Cornwall, but clearer and more explicit is a section of what he called 'The Reality of Peace' which he wrote once he was there. Here he adopts a more favourable view of dissolution, comparing it to the breaking down and decay which has to take place in Nature before new life can appear, but also to the alimentary functions of the body. 'Within our bowels flows the slow stream of corruption, to the issue of corruption. This is one direction. Within our veins flows the stream of life, towards the issue of pure creation. This is the other direction. We are both'. What Lawrence wants to insist on is acceptance of both processes, that we should live 'not by exclusion, but by incorporation and unison'. And that we should not feel ashamed that we are constituted in this dual fashion:

> Is it a pride in me that in my blood the fire flickers out of the wheaten bread I have partaken of? ... Then how shall it be a shame that from my blood exudes the bitter sweat

of corruption on the journey back to dissolution; how shall it be a shame that in my consciousness appear the heavy marsh-flowers of the flux of putrescence, which have their natural roots in the slow stream of decomposition that flows for ever down my bowels?[45]

It is among those 'heavy marsh-flowers' of his consciousness that Lawrence locates what he calls the 'serpent of secret and shameful desire'. What is important is that this serpent should not be beaten 'out of my consciousness with sticks' because, in that case, 'it will lie beyond, in the marsh of the so-called subconsciousness':

Let me bring it to the fire to see what is. For a serpent is a thing created. It has its own *raison d'être*. In its own being it has beauty and reality. Even my horror is a tribute to its reality. And I must admit the genuineness of my horror, accept it, and not exclude it from my understanding.[46]

Lawrence does not say what his own 'secret and shameful' desires are although the context suggest that they are closely associated with excrement and the anus. What he provides instead is his own, heavily metaphorical account of why repression is wrong and what he suggests is that he has looked into his own nature and (unlike the Birkin of the 'Prologue') determined to accept what is there. To complain that he is not as clear as one might like is perhaps not very fair in that there were other texts from this period (*Goats and Compasses*, *At the Gates*) where we can infer he struggled further with these issues, but which have disappeared. His general stance he did however describe in very direct language in a letter he wrote to Eunice Tietjens, shortly after he had written 'The Reality of Peace': 'Desire is from the unknown which is the Creator and Destroyer, beyond us, that which precedes us and brings us into being. Therefore desire is holy, belonging to the mystic unknown, no matter *what* the desire'.[47] No desire, that is, which is genuine and not mind-generated (like incest craving) can be wrong, a principle which was far from his mind when he was denouncing the homosexuality of Keynes, Birrell and Garnett.

Varieties of love

Birkin hopes that his intimate relation with Ursula in *Women in Love* will be complemented by an equally intimate one with Gerald, but this never happens. That he should need an alternative might seem only reasonable if one imagines him familiar with her previous sexual history as it is described in the latter half of *The Rainbow*, which of course he could not be since *Women in Love* is in no proper sense the sequel Lawrence once described it as being.[48] After various struggles with love and sex in that earlier novel, Ursula eventually becomes engaged to an army officer called Anton Skrebensky whose origins are Polish but whose attitudes are conventionally British, especially as regards his acceptance of any war in which he might be called upon to fight. Despite Ursula's fierce criticism of him for this, which must have been offensive to many when the novel was published in 1915, she nevertheless seems to become reconciled to marrying Anton. The idea is that she will join him later at his overseas posting in India but, before that, he is obliged by her to go for a walk along a beach where, under a bright moon, she intends to make love (the society she has been brought up being, at this stage in *The Rainbow*, far more 'advanced' than her grandfather's had been).

> Then there, in the great flare of light, she clinched hold of him, hard, as if suddenly she had the strength of destruction, she fastened her arms around him and tightened him in her grip, whilst her mouth sought his in a hard, rending, ever-increasing kiss, till his body was powerless in her grip, his heart melted in fear from the fierce, beaked harpy's kiss.[49]

This may be the first but it is certainly not the last time a reader of Lawrence will hear of the beaked harpy as a representative of ravenous female desire. In most of the novel, much of Ursula's experience is told from her point of view, but here the focus switches to the male who is her victim, especially when Ursula leads Skrebensky to a slope which lies 'full under the moonshine':

> He came direct to her, without preliminaries. She held him pinned down at the chest, awful. The fight, the struggle for consummation was terrible. It lasted till it was agony to his soul, till he succumbed, till he gave way as if dead, and lay with his face buried partly in her hair partly in the sand, motionless, as if he would be motionless now for ever, hidden away in the dark, buried, only buried, he only wanted to be buried in the goodly darkness, only that, no more.
>
> He seemed to swoon. It was a long time before he came to himself. He was aware of an unusual motion of her breast. He looked up. Her face lay like an image in the moonlight, the eyes wide open, rigid. But out of the eyes, slowly, there rolled a tear, that glittered in the moonlight as it ran down her cheek.
>
> He felt as if the knife were being pushed into his already dead body.

Before this passage we have been told that Skrebensky felt the 'ordeal of proof' was upon him.[50] Whether or not that is the demand he should sexually satisfy Ursula, what is clear is that he has failed a test and that the two of them will not be married after all. The general point is that the sexual intercourse from which characters elsewhere in Lawrence expect so much does not here deliver, and is in fact no more than a deeply unpleasant experience for the male involved (and perhaps for the female also).

Ursula and Gudrun, the female protagonists of *Women in Love*, are what were called at the time 'new women' in a world recognisably even more modern than that of the latter half of *The Rainbow*, and with a different attitude to sexual relations. Writing and then re-writing the novel during the war, Lawrence was unusually percipient in realising how radically English society would have changed by the end of it: how many traditions and habits would have been swept away. As an artist, Gudrun is the more obviously avant-garde, having mixed in London with the same bohemian set which Birkin frequents from time to time. There is nothing 'Victorian' in her attitude to sex even though, when the novel opens, she is back living with her parents in the Midlands. Both those facts about her are made clear in the episode where she accepts Gerald Crich into her bed after he has crept into her family home at night. What drives him to this desperate measure is distress at the recent loss of his father, and the sex he is looking for from Gudrun is quite patently what is now known as the comfort variety:

> He buried his small, hard head between her breasts, and pressed her breasts against him with his hands. And she with quivering hands pressed his head against her, as he lay suffused out, and she lay fully conscious. The lovely, creative warmth flooded through him like a sleep of fecundity within the womb. Ah if only she would grant him this living effluence, he would be restored, he would be complete again. He was afraid she would deny him before it was finished. Like a child at the breast, he cleaved intensely to her, and she could not put him away.[51]

This was the kind of maternal comfort which Frieda appeared often ready to provide to young men who, like Lawrence when she first met him, were inexperienced and uncertain about their sexuality. Very early on, when he was separated from her in Germany, and she was tormenting him with references to a young army officer she might help out of his emotional difficulties, he reminded her of the story by Maupassant in which a wet nurse suckles a young Italian workman. Since the nurse's breasts are hurting because they are full of milk, and the soldier has not eaten in a long time, both parties are happy when they take leave of each other; but Lawrence suggested the exchange was not 'manly',[52] and he must have felt that he had not escaped his own mother only to find another. Besides, in the passage from *Women in Love* above, only one of the two participants in the encounter finds it satisfying. Not an especially maternal woman (very early in the novel she expresses her distaste for having children), Gudrun is described a little later in this scene as 'destroyed into perfect consciousness, …with wide eyes staring motionless into the darkness'.[53] This mode of the writing is continuous with that in *The Rainbow* although, in general, *Women in Love* is a quite different reading experience. Dealing as it does with highly educated people, it consists largely of the animated discussion of ideas interspersed with descriptions of apparently random events invested with a significance it is reasonable to call symbolic.

Two of these events, much earlier in the novel than Gerald's night-time visit to Gudrun, help to explain why he is not *just* like a child seeking its mother, and why she should be so interested in him. In the first of these she watches fascinated when he forces his panic-stricken Arab mare to stand by a railway crossing as a train clatters noisily by, and is especially excited by the way he digs his spurs into the animal's sides until the blood flows. In the second, she is with him when, at the expense of what is this time some of his own blood, he subdues a wildly struggling buck rabbit. Both these well-known episodes dimly suggest the kind of enjoyment the masochist might derive from witnessing examples of sadism; and that, when he is not seeking maternal comfort, Gerald can be something of a sadist in his sexual relations is hinted at after Birkin has taken him to London to meet some of his own bohemian artist friends. There Gerald ends up sleeping with a young model known as the Pussum. 'She seemed to flow back, almost like liquid, from his approach', Lawrence writes, 'to sink helplessly away from him. Her inchoate look of a violated slave, whose fulfilment lies in her further and further violation, made his nerves quiver with acutely desirable sensation'.[54] These words do not however mean that the Pussum is in any sense a victim of Gerald, any more that Gudrun will be (in the scene with the rabbit, she is described as looking at Gerald with the eyes of 'a creature which is at his mercy, yet which is his ultimate victor').[55] Both these women have the advantage over him of knowing what they are looking for in a relationship, and who they are. They are more powerful than Gerald because he is at the mercy of his instincts, ignorant of his true nature, whereas they are able to manipulate and control them.

Gudrun leads Gerald into a world of sensation-seeking, so that they can (as it were) carry on from the stage at which, as far as their sexual life is concerned, Will and Anna are last seen in *The Rainbow*. It is true that his wealth and his power in the world of men, where he is a mine owner, adds to his appeal; but very soon he proves an inadequate partner for her, too heavy, unsophisticated and naïve. She recognises a more fitting mate in the German artist Loerke whose attitude to sexuality is indicated by the statuette he has made of a naked, pubescent young girl draped astride a huge horse, her bare, slight, vulnerable legs reaching down its powerful flanks. Lawrence was dealing with these matters only a decade after Krafft-Ebing had published his *Psychopathia Sexualis* and Havelock Ellis his *Studies in the Psychology of Sex;* and when Freud was busy elaborating the idea that all infants are polymorphously perverse, seeking erotic satisfaction in many different parts of the body before concentrating, for the most part, on the genitalia. What many would have called aberrations, and some perversions, of the sexual instincts, are treated by Lawrence with great subtlety, and some sympathy. But the attitude he is inclined to take up is in part determined by his controlling metaphor.

That is of course the river of dissolution, the drift down which tends to be associated with marshes, putrescence (which can have its own phosphorescent beauty), rats and snakes. This means that although being carried by that river is a necessary process before fresh new life can begin, and one in which we must all partake, the feelings of what goes on in the interim have an inevitable pejorative tinge. The problem is that some people (like Gudrun and Loerke) are not particularly concerned with moving on, but enjoy the often exquisite sensations which can be associated with dissolution and decay. It is significant that the statuette not only reveals Loerke's sadistic side but that, when he first appears, Lawrence presents him as bisexual. All the writing which involves Gudrun is powerful because it seems to be written with such remarkable understanding and inwardness. But Birkin wants something both different and better that he hopes he will find with Ursula.

LOVE TRIUMPHANT?

What Ursula offers Birkin is the salvation of her 'love', just as Paula had in 'New Eve and Old Adam'. The moment is important in Lawrence's writing in that the whole idea of love now comes under an attack from Birkin much more sustained than it was in the story. In the scene in *The Rainbow* which begins with Ursula's predatory kissing of Skrebensky, moonlight is a crucial element, starkly illuminating Skrebensky's failure. It figures significantly also in *Women in Love*, notably in the chapter of which the very title is 'Moony'. This begins with Birkin repeatedly throwing stones into a pond in order to break up the moon's reflection on its surface although with a success that, in the nature of things, can only ever be temporary. Normally there is some discomfort in using the heavy term 'symbolic' for scenes of this kind in *Women in Love*, but here it is made absolutely plain that the moon represents the female principle, the threat of women: 'Cybele – curse her!', Birkin mutters, 'The accursed Syria Dea! – Does one begrudge her? – What else is there?'[56] Women may have initially represented for Lawrence an escape from self-enclosure and made him feel, in his more optimistic moments, that sex was a process which could lead to greater self-realisation, a clarifying of one's otherwise discordant elements which constitutes a form of a rebirth. But the danger of the absorption into another's nature, in what he often liked to call 'lapsing out', is that the weaker party may become disorientated and lose individuality. In a scene where Birkin has come to Gerald to complain about Ursula, he says he wants 'so much to be free, not under the compulsion of any need for unification'; that he would like 'to be with Ursula as free as with himself, single and clear and cool, yet balanced, polarised with her. The merging, the clutching, the mingling of love', Lawrence observes, 'was becoming madly abhorrent to him':

> But it seemed to him, woman was always so horrible and clutching, she had such a lust for possession, a greed of self-importance in love. She wanted to have, to own, to control, to be dominant. Everything must be referred back to her, to Woman, the great Mother of everything, out of whom proceeded everything and to whom everything must finally be rendered up.
>
> It filled him with almost insane fury, this calm assumption of the Magna Mater, that all was hers, because she had borne it.[57]

This is only one of Birkin's often contradictory moods, and certainly there is built into *Women in Love* a good deal of criticism of both them and him. One of the abiding images of the novel nevertheless comes after the lake around which a 'water party' has recently been held is dredged because two of those present have drowned. A daughter of the hosts is one of the victims and, when they find her body, she has her arms tightly clasped around the neck of the young doctor who had jumped into the water in order to try and save her.

It is Birkin's suspicion of Ursula, and of the nature of the love she offers, which makes him gravitate towards Gerald. Yet although

Gerald takes the naked wrestling in his stride and admits he has never felt as much love for a woman as he does for Birkin, he is sceptical as to what that might mean. When Birkin talks again of an '*additional* perfect relationship between man and man – additional to marriage', Gerald objects that 'Nature doesn't provide the basis'. 'Well, of course, I think she does' his friend replies[58] without (as far as one can tell) endorsing the homosexuality which is stigmatised in the initial description of Loerke's arrival on the scene with a young male friend, or (more clearly) in the previous account in *The Rainbow* of Ursula's brief affair with her lesbian schoolteacher.

To avoid what he finds disturbing in Ursula's notion of love, Birkin offers his conception of 'stellar polarity'. This is the idea that a couple could be like two stars confirmed in their singleness by the gravitational forces which hold them in unison and prevent them from crashing into one another. Several critics have succeeded in making better sense of this image than Birkin himself does, but then he is a character in a novel struggling to find his way. On one relatively early occasion when he is expounding stellar polarity to Ursula, they are interrupted by the sight of his cat stalking a female intruder round the garden and cuffing her from time to time with his paw. Ursula is not presented in the novel as an intellectual – she hates 'subtleties', regarding them as 'a sign of weakness'[59] – but when Birkin is tempted to offer the cats as an illustration of his general position, it does not take much intellect to point out that they are not a particularly pleasing example of 'stable equilibrium'. What they rather suggest is that tendency in Lawrence himself, which was to become much stronger later, to recognise that, for him, love (and here the term can and indeed must be taken to include sex) is always a conflict in which there has to be a winner or loser.

The dilemma for Ursula and Birkin – as Birkin sees it – is to avoid the situation Gerald and Gudrun find themselves in: 'the eternal see-saw, one destroyed that the other might exist, one ratified because the other was nulled'.[60] Lawrence wants to suggest that Birkin and Ursula manage to do this so that his final willingness to accept her love, and admit he loves her, is not the defeat it might otherwise seem. The crucial work goes on in the chapter called 'Excurse', over which a great deal of ink has been spilled. Near its beginning, Birkin complains that, 'He had taken [Ursula] as he had never been taken himself. He had taken her at the roots of her darkness and shame – like a demon, laughing over the fountain of mystic corruption which was one of the sources of her being …'[61] If this is, as many justifiably feel, another allusion to anal intercourse then one might reasonably object with Gerald that Nature does not provide the means for Ursula taking Birkin as he has taken her. Yet shortly after these reflections, the two find themselves before the open fire in the parlour of a coaching inn waiting to be served high tea. Admirers of Lawrence, aware of the many several different kinds of writing in which he excels, and annoyed by how little his variety is generally recognised, might well prefer merely to summarise what follows so that for them it will only seem unfortunate that the passages concerned are unsummarisable, and can only be quoted in full. Ursula has knelt down in front of Birkin on the hearth rug, embraced him and cried 'My love', to which Birkin has responded with identical words:

> She closed her hands over the full, rounded body of his loins, as he stooped over her, she seemed to touch the quick of the mystery of darkness that was bodily him. She seemed to faint beneath, and he seemed to faint, stooping over her. It was a perfect passing away for both of them, and at the same time the most intolerable accession into being, the marvellous fullness of immediate gratification, overwhelming, outflooding from the Source of the deepest life-force, the darkest, deepest strangest life-source of the human body, at the back and base of the loins.

It is important that both the participants in this episode are fully clothed, and will shortly be partaking of the delights of an English high tea ('What *good* things!', Ursula exclaims). All that helps to make the epiphany they experience before the tea is served, that 'perfect passing away' which is also an 'accession into being' or rebirth, more puzzling; and the longer paragraph which immediately follows is scarcely more enlightening:

> After a lapse of stillness, after the rivers of strange dark fluid richness had passed over her, flooding, carrying away her mind and flooding down her spine and down her knees, past her feet, a strange flood, sweeping away everything and leaving her an essential new being, she was left quite free, she was free in complete ease, her complete self. So she rose, stilly and blithe, smiling at him. He stood before her, glimmering, so awfully real, that her heart almost stopped beating. He stood there in his strange, whole body, that had its marvellous fountains, like the bodies of the Sons of God who were in the beginning. There were strange fountains of his body, more mysterious and potent than any she had imagined or known, more satisfying, ah, finally, mystically-physically satisfying. She had thought there was no source deeper than the phallic source. And, now, behold, from the smitten rock of the man's body, from the strange marvellous flanks and thighs, deeper, further in mystery than the phallic source, came the floods of ineffable darkness and ineffable riches.[62]

It was while he was writing *Women in Love* that Lawrence had become interested in a number of writings which could be broadly termed 'theosophical', and which display a strong interest in yoga and eastern philosophy generally. The one from which he took the idea of body centres (or chakras), and used as a rival to the Freudian topography in his second book on psychoanalysis and the unconscious, was by James Pryce and called *The Apocalypse Unsealed*; yet it was Lawrence himself who decided that the most important chakra lay at the base of the spine. This may help to explain why that part of the body figures so centrally in these passages, but not the repeated emphasis on the release of fluids. These are associated more with Birkin than with Ursula and, since the phallus as an origin is explicitly excluded, can only be metaphorical. But what quite is this satisfaction Birkin provides Ursula which is both deeper and further in mystery than the phallic source?

Readers might hope they may discover the answer to that question when Ursula and Birkin leave the coaching inn and drive to a spot in the woods where they can finally make love. What they excitedly anticipate will be the result of their love-making is the 'star equilibrium which alone is freedom':

> They threw off their clothes, and he gathered her to him, and found her, found the pure lambent reality of her forever invisible flesh. Quenched, inhuman, his fingers upon her unrevealed nudity were the fingers of silence upon silence, the body of mysterious night upon the body of mysterious night, the night masculine and feminine, never to be seen with the eye, or known with the mind, only known as a palpable revelation of living otherness.
>
> She had her desire of him, she touched, she received the maximums of unspeakable communication in touch, dark, subtle, positively silent, a magnificent gift and give again, a perfect acceptance and yielding, a mystery, the reality of that which can never be known, vital, sensual reality that can never be transmuted into mind content, but remains outside, living body of darkness and silence and subtlety, the mystic body of reality. She had her desire fulfilled, he had his desire fulfilled. For she was to him what he was to her,

the immemorial magnificence of mystic, palpable, real otherness.[63]

From a thematic point of view, these two paragraphs are among the most important in *Women in Love*; but to my mind they are also among the worst Lawrence ever wrote. It is his evident intention to set against the bleak tragedy of Gerald's failure with Gudrun, so memorably and tellingly recounted, the more positive outcome of the relationship between Ursula and Birkin. The only thing we learn here is that the two have managed to be intimate while at the same time remaining aware of each one's 'otherness'. Why that should be so is a mystery enveloped in the worst kind of windy rhetoric. How best to describe sexual intercourse is of course a peculiarly difficult problem for Lawrence, especially in the publishing conditions of his day, and it was one with which he struggled throughout his career. Here he seems to have decided that it sometimes involves a reality 'which can never be known', but in that case it would surely have been better to say so more plainly and without recourse to vague terms of empty, hectoring assertion. The effect of these is to leave the reader baffled but also sceptically aware that, if *this* is how Birkin's anxieties have been assuaged, there is no guarantee that they will not reappear. That is suspicion which Lawrence does not give readers an opportunity to confirm within the context of *Women in Love* itself but, insofar as those anxieties are a reflection of Lawrence's own, it is more than borne out by his treatment of love and sex in the works which followed. Critics often refer to Lawrence's 'dialectic' yet although he is an instinctive and habitual dualist, always pitting one term against its contrary, his syntheses are (in my view) rarely convincing, or at least no more so than they are in the passages from 'Excurse' quoted here.

Chapter Three:
The road to disillusion

Whitman

[handwritten note: Nerve centres]

I f the encounter between Ursula and Birkin in *Women in Love*,
when they are in front of an inn fire and waiting for their tea
to be brought, is barely comprehensible, it seems to me that
it is not comprehensible *at all* without some knowledge of Lawrence's interest in body or nerve centres. Although he had first been
made aware of these in 1917, his *Fantasia of the Unconscious*, in
which they are so important, was not published until 1921; but in
the intervening period they had remained a prominent part of this
thinking (as *Women in Love* illustrates). They figure significantly,
for example, in the essays on the great American writers which
he began composing while he was still in Cornwall and eventually published as *Studies in Classic American Literature*. Alternately
profound and eccentric, these essays concern figures such as Cooper, Hawthorne, Melville and Poe but perhaps the most personally
important to Lawrence was Whitman whose influence on him
stretches back well beyond the war years. It was after all Whitman who had helped him to throw off the shackles of regular verse
forms (which he rarely handled well), and to adopt free verse in his
poetry; but he was also well known as the poet of manly love, the
love of comrades. Lawrence's essay on him went through several
stages but in one of these, written in 1919, his concern with body
centres is very much in evidence. One of Whitman's weaknesses,
Lawrence claims, is that he concentrated too much on the out-go-
ing and sympathetic chakras in the front of the upper torso, always
wanting to find his reality in 'Allness or infinitude' and merge with
the outside world. Yet there are of course two kinds of merging:
one in which what is other is incorporated into the self, and its
obverse in which there is the 'ecstasy of acute physical passing away

... in a self-loss keen and delirious as death or sheer delight'. The problem with the latter is that 'a man cannot endlessly merge into all things without endlessly departing from his own integral self'. Lawrence appears to find a model for thinking about relations with what is other, and with other people especially, in electricity. When these relations are 'deep and passional', there is, according to him, a 'vital circuit' which has its negative and positive 'poles of establish-ment' in the chakras. Coming on to those lower centres which he is suggesting Whitman too much ignored, he insists that there is one even lower than those he had found in Pryce (the plexuses or nerve centres he mentions do of course exist so that it is only the use he makes of them which is pseudo-scientific):

> The vagina, as we know, is the orifice to the hypogastric plexus, which, in the old words, 'is situated amid the wa-ters'. It is the advent to the great source of being, and it is the egress of the bitter, spent waters of the end. But beyond all this is the cocygeal centre. There the deepest and most unknowable sensual reality breathes and sparkles darkly, in unspeakable power. Here, at the root of the spine, is the last clue to the lower body and being, as in the cerebellum is the last upper clue. ... And the port, of egress and ingress, is the fundament, as the vagina is port to the other centre.[1]

If the hypogastric plexus is the clue to the 'bitter, departing waters of the end' (by which Lawrence presumably means urine), so the coxygeal, usually spelt with two 'c's and the nerve centre closest to what is popularly called the tailbone, is the clue to

> the fiery corruption which is also the stream of our be-ing. As the circuit between man and woman embraces the stream of watery corruption, so does the other circuit em-brace the stream of fiery corruption, which we have been so

afraid to know: and with which Rabelais, and many other humorists, have mocked us.[2]

Always clearly implied when Lawrence talks about 'the circuit between man and woman' here is the sexual act, which in the same section of this essay is made responsible for 'the forever-refreshing establishment and readjustment of the circuit of life'. But if 'the last mystery of established polarity' is 'between the poles of the cocygeal centres' then it follows, as far as he is concerned, that '*the last perfect balance is between two men*, in whom the deepest sensual centres, and also the extreme upper centres, vibrate in one circuit' (my italics). This must not be a merging, as it too often is in Whitman: 'The true relation rests on an established polarity, where one being indeed is negative in his polarity, but where both maintain their sheer single, separate integrity, their inviolable singleness of being' (which is Birkin's 'stellar polarity' expressed in different terms). The weakness of Whitman was that he believed in merging, or 'fusion – which is pure loss'. Greek pederasty was, Lawrence claims, 'a form of fusion, or merging'. This was because the lover 'caught his beloved at the nascent point of adolescence …the one being possessed utterly the other …There was no equality, no equilibrised duality, no delicately-suspended true polarity'.[3] The way in which he offers this qualification, without that is condemning homosexuality as such, would seem to confirm that the circuit he is thinking of when he talks of the relations between men is indeed primarily a matter of sex.

If these tortuous passages are not an explicit endorsement of sexual intercourse between men, they come very close to it. The difference between them and what Lawrence had said in his letter to Garnett after his Cambridge visit is striking, but then a lot had happened in the meantime. Once Lawrence had settled in Cornwall he became very friendly and indeed, as the account he later gave of the relationship in *Kangaroo* shows, fell in love with the son of a local farmer.[4] What he seems to have attempted, as the two men worked in the fields together, is a recreation of the conditions of his early friendship with Alan Chambers although, as in that case, it seems highly unlikely that he had, or attempted to have, sex with his Cornish friend. This was, however, at the same time as he was writing that all genuine desires must be openly acknowledged, and all of them are holy. Understanding himself better may have been one reason why his attitude towards intercourse between men softened, even if there was too much in his own upbringing and temperament to make it possible in his own case. And then of course there would always have been Frieda to insist, as Ursula does in *Women in Love*, that anything of that nature was a perversity.[5]

For Lawrence to have eventually reached a position, if only in one unpublished text, which might now be described by many as enlightened is nevertheless significant, although it would be hard to avoid the charge that what is going on in the Whitman essay amounts to desperate rationalisation. In his letter to Savage, he had said that 'one is kept by all tradition and instinct from loving men, or a man'. The very least that could be said of the structure he seems to feel obliged to put in place in order to overcome this tradition (if not instinct) is that it is curiously elaborate. Why, moreover, it should be the cocygeal centre where 'the deepest and most unknowable sensual reality breathes and sparkles darkly, in unspeakable power' is not clear. The choice seems related less to any natural hierarchies in the body than to the anus as a dual source of both attraction and repulsion. One could of course say that the whole system of body centres is no more than a useful device Lawrence adopted in order to emphasise how, in modern life, people had become far too cerebral and allowed the more instinctual parts of their natures to atrophy ('Be a good animal' was the advice of the gamekeeper Annabel in *The White Peacock*).[6] It certainly does that, yet it was never just a device for Lawrence but something he believed in literally. The idea of relationships between people being like an electrical circuit is, on the other hand, self-consciously metaphorical but runs into problems of which he himself makes us aware. His whole complicated scenario appears to be designed to allow himself to feel that the sexual element in his feeling for men was not only legitimate but superior to the sexual feeling he had for women. Yet he makes clear that the circuit he is thinking of as establishing relationships must have both a positive and negative pole (or what would more normally be called terminals). Although he wants to insist that, despite this talk of negative and positive, there can be sexual relations between men which leave both feeling independent and equal, the very language he uses suggests that, were he ever to have indulged in sexual relations with a man, he would have found waiting for him the same difficulties of domination and submission which he had encountered in his relationship with Frieda.

THE LOST GIRL

If the progress of Lawrence's own feelings about love and sex are not easy to track through his writings it is because, in the first place, they do not develop in a conveniently orderly or linear fashion and, in the second, many of those writings are revised so often that they become palimpsests, with each layer representative of a different phase in his life. A typical example is the novel which was eventually entitled *The Lost Girl*. He had begun a version of this work when he was in Germany in 1913 but it had been left behind on his return to England. He was only able to recover the copy after the war so that, rewritten, it was 1920 before it was finally published. When he began the novel Lawrence was worried that its theme would make it improper since it dealt with a topic much discussed at that time: what to do about the large number of middle-class women for whom there were not enough suitable husbands, and who failed (or refused!) to marry. Although in his second novel, *The Trespasser*, one has to look hard to discover whether the two main characters do in fact have sexual intercourse on the Isle of Wight, it was nevertheless focussed squarely on adultery. At that stage, he was anxious not to acquire too much of a reputation as a writer of improper books which might damage his commercial prospects. When he began to rewrite *The Lost Girl* in 1920, after the banning of *The Rainbow* and his struggles to get *Women in Love* into print, he was still desperately short of money and even more anxious therefore to produce something that would sell. To a certain degree he was successful. Although he had to undertake some revision before it could appear, that there was no special storm of protest to accompany the publication of *The Lost Girl* is suggested by its having won the James Tait Black Memorial Prize for the best novel of its year.

The heroine of the novel, Alvina Houghton, is the daughter of an initially prosperous shopkeeper in a town in the English Midlands which Lawrence calls Woodhouse, and its relative success must have been in large part owing to the vividness with which her social background is evoked. In a realist mode which he largely abandoned for parts of his career but which always remained at his disposal, he displays a good deal of satirical verve in tracking the progress of Alvina's father from prosperity to destitution as he engages in one madcap commercial scheme after another. The last of these is a large marquee or tent in which live actors operate alternately with flickering silent films. One of these actors is a southern Italian called Ciccio who is part of a troupe which performs short dramatic sketches and Red Indian dances. Although he is completely without what in Woodhouse would be called culture, and has a level of English which makes it difficult for Alvina to communicate with him, Ciccio is more appealing to her than any of the young men who had previously appeared in her restricted circle. When her father dies, she loses status almost immediately by deciding to join Ciccio's travelling troupe and play the piano for them. This leads to an unpleasant scene in which she is more or less coerced into sleeping with him, but she has misgivings about a permanent relationship and retreats back to Woodhouse. When Ciccio visits Alvina there she is happy to have him stay in the family house, despite the social solecism that represents, but reluctant to allow him into her bed. This behaviour both puzzles and exasperates Ciccio whose frustration precipitates violence in a scene which, had Lawrence not bowed to pressure from his publisher and completely rewritten it for the version of the novel which appeared in England in 1920, might well have made the Edinburgh academics pause before awarding him the James Tait prize:

> For a second, she struggled frenziedly. But almost instantly she recognised how much stronger he was, and she was still, mute and motionless with anger. White, and mute, and motionless, she was taken to her room. At the back of her mind all the time she wondered at his deliberate recklessness of her. Recklessly, he had his will of her – but deliberately, and thoroughly, not rushing to the issue, but taking everything he wanted of her, progressively, and fully, leaving her stark, with nothing, nothing of herself – nothing.
>
> When she could lie still she turned away from him, still mute. And he lay with his arms over her, motionless. Noises went on, in the street, overhead in the workroom. But theirs was complete silence.
>
> At last he rose and looked at her.
>
> 'Love is a fine thing, Allaye', he said. [Allaye being the name she has been given in the troupe].
>
> She lay mute and unmoving. He approached, laid his hand on her breast, and kissed her.
>
> 'Love', he said, asserting, and laughing.
>
> But still she was completely mute and motionless. He threw bedclothes over her and went downstairs, whistling softly.

Ciccio is someone who has no trouble working out how love and sex interact since for him they are synonymous terms; yet what he does to Alvina would by most people be described as rape. How far her not quite seeing it that way can be ascribed to a male author having adopted her point of view will be a matter for individual judgement. The passage below follows on immediately from the one above:

> She knew she would have to break her own trance of obsti-
> nacy. So she struggled down into her bedclothes, shivering
> deliciously, for her skin had become chilled. She didn't care
> a bit, really, about her own downfall. She snuggled deli-
> ciously in the sheets., and admitted to herself that she loved
> him. In truth, she loved him – and she was laughing to
> herself.[7]

Lawrence's idea here seems to be that it was only Alvina's conventional upbringing which had initiated her stop/go strategy with
Ciccio, and that she is grateful for having it swept away now so
forcibly: that his violence allows her to be finally true to her real
nature. Yet in the fiction Lawrence went on to write after this there
is a disturbing number of similar examples of women being over-
powered by men, and often being reduced to slavish dependence,
which might make one suspect the lurking presence in the author
of a sexual fantasy of compensation which distorts the narrative and
leaves the reader wondering whether a male author is really qualified to know whether a woman would respond as (for instance)
Alvina does in this case. Novelists are of course free to do whatever
they like with characters they themselves have created, but not if –
according to critical criteria Lawrence himself did much to make
current – they contradict a previously established emotional logic
in order to satisfy their own half-conscious predilections.

Dramatic as it is, this episode in *The Lost Girl* is not the most
important one for my subject. Alvina rejoins Ciccio's troupe but
because her bankrupt father has left her no money, she feels herself
a drag on its resources and applies for a job as a midwife in Lan-
caster. Her life there is very effectively described and includes a
splendid if repulsive portrait of a middle-aged doctor who, having

worked hard to establish himself, decides it is time to marry and picks the much younger Alvina as a suitable future wife. He represents both status and security so that, although not in the least attracted physically, she allows herself to become engaged to him. Meanwhile she is asked to attend on a local woman called Effie Tuke who is pregnant and reaching her term. In an extraordinary scene, this woman's labour pains begin while outside her large house Ciccio, who has not previously been represented as love-lorn, suddenly appears and is heard singing a Neapolitan love song full of desperate yearning. 'Oh, the flesh is a beastly thing!', Effie says, 'To make a man howl outside there like that, because you're here. – And to make me howl because I've got a child inside me'. As the situation develops and becomes increasingly intolerable, she draws conclusions from it which are more philosophical:

> 'Nurse!', cried Effie. 'It's *no use* trying to get a grip on life. – You're just at the mercy of *Forces,*' she shrieked angrily.
> 'Why not?', said Alvina. 'There are good life-forces. Even the will of God is a life-force.'
> 'You don't understand! I want to be *myself.* And I'm *not* myself. I'm just torn to pieces by *Forces.* It's horrible – '
> 'Well, it's not my fault. I didn't make the universe,' said Alvina. 'If you have to be torn to pieces by forces, well, you have. Other forces will put you together again.'
> 'I don't want them to. I want to be myself. I don't want to be nailed together like a chair, with a hammer. I want to be myself.'
> 'You won't be nailed together like a chair. – You should have faith in life.'[8]

The view Effie expresses here is identical to Schopenhauer's: the sexual forces which have brought about her pregnancy, and which are producing Ciccio's 'despairing howl' outside her window, have no regard whatsoever for the individuals who are their channels. Alvina's response to Effie's Schopenhaurean misery is 'faith in life'. She ignores her engagement to the middle-aged doctor and agrees to marry Ciccio who, since the war has broken out and his troupe has been disbanded, takes her back to his family home in that mountainous region south of Naples known as the Abruzzi. But there it is mid-winter and very cold, and the living conditions are remarkably primitive. She has no company and, culturally speaking, is a complete fish out of water, with only the physical relation with Ciccio to sustain her. When Italy enters the war and he decides to enlist, she is faced with the prospect of having the child she is now carrying in an environment which is entirely alien, and without the support of a husband whose return from the war must be doubtful. Although she has committed herself to 'life', prioritising sexual attraction over everything else, the least that can be said is that her faith in it will be severely tested. This is a conclusion forced on readers by the way the ending of *The Lost Girl* is written and, on Lawrence's own principle of never trusting the teller but the tale, it suggests that his own rejection of Effie and Schopenhauer's pessimism is not as firm and definite as his reputation as a Nietzschean life-affirmer might lead one to expect.

ROSALIND BAYNES

There is some fine descriptive writing at the end of *The Lost Girl* as Ciccio and Alvina make their way to the Abruzzi and settle in there. This is a direct consequence of Lawrence and Frieda having themselves visited the area in December 1919, very shortly after they had at last been able to leave England. During the war they had received a good deal of kindness from a woman called Rosalind Baynes. Once the war was over, she was anxious to transport herself, her three children and a nurse to Italy while the proceedings which would lead to a divorce from her husband were taking place. An Italian who had been a model for her sculptor father had offered the use of a house he owned in the small Abruzzi village of Picinisco and the Lawrences agreed that they would check it out. Since this is the building which provides the model for Ciccio's house in *The Lost Girl*, it is no surprise for anyone who reads the novel that Lawrence should have told Rosalind Baynes that, beautiful though the surrounding countryside might be, it was unsuitable for her needs. He himself did not stay long but quickly moved on to Capri, and other more comfortable places, before settling for a while in Taormina in Sicily. This was a time when he wrote some of his best poems, those which he later collected together under the title *Birds, Beasts and Flowers*: effective and beautiful evocations of the natural world he found around him in Italy, its flora but (and perhaps even more memorably) its fauna also. Several of these were written on a trip back north to Florence in 1920, when Lawrence was camping in a huge, deserted villa, close to where Rosalind Baynes had eventually found a temporary home. This was while he was waiting to rejoin Frieda who had gone to visit her relatives in Germany so that it is Baynes who provides us with the only existing, reliable evidence of a consummated, extra-marital affair involving Lawrence.

Baynes's testimony may of course be false, but what makes that unlikely is the conversation she records, in a private memoir never meant for publication, as leading up to her sleeping with Lawrence. That she was separated from her husband, and about to divorce, had led Lawrence to ask how she felt without sex in her life. When she replied that sex was something she did indeed miss, he suggested that a husband was not after all the only solution. This inviting remark caused her to say that the difficulty lay in being 'so damned fastidious'. She reports Lawrence as then insisting that he could not agree more and that one could hardly bear to come near to most people, never mind make love to them. The difficulty, she then went on, was that it was no use just having sex, 'a few pretty words then off to bed'. Agreeing again, Lawrence added a highly characteristic proviso:

> Yes there must be more in it than that, but God save us
> from the so-called Love – the most indecent kind of egoism
> and self-spreading. Let us think of love as a force outside
> and getting us. It is a force, a god …

These remarks begin with a usefully blunt summary of Lawrence's
objection to love, which he dramatises in *Women in Love* and elsewhere, and it is not surprising to find his definition of the word
being followed by the allusion to an outside force to which we
have to yield, and which is referred to as a god (the 'will of God'
is what Alvina had called it). In Schopenhauer's 'The Metaphysics
of Love', the outside force is the reproductive urge implanted in all
Nature and he consistently defines all sexual desire by its assumed
origins in that urge, and then all love by its origins in sexual desire.
This is a general style of thinking which is reductive, as Lawrence
himself had implicitly suggested in some remarks about poppies at
the beginning of *The Study of Thomas Hardy*.[9] The real or imagined
origins of a phenomenon do not always tell us what we may most
want or need to know about it. Tracing Holy Communion back to
human sacrifice, for example, could only ever be minimally illuminating, even for non-believers.

Lawrence wants Rosalind Baynes to think of what will shortly
take place between them as a godly outside force which 'gets' them,
without their conscious participation. But her response is both
shrewd and commonsensical. After all, they have just been talking
of how fastidious they both are but how can that be if, she asks,
'there is no personalism in love'. Oh yes, Lawrence airily replies,
'there must be understanding of the god *together*' (a principle of
which Ciccio had clearly not been informed). Although 'personalism' is not perhaps the best word for Baynes to have included in
her question, the answer she receives is hardly adequate. There is
after all a host of particularities that make one person attractive to
another: love usually has to begin with something attractive in the
object loved, and Baynes might reasonably be wondering whether

she possesses any of these, whether in fact Lawrence actually *likes* rather than just desires her (a question that certainly occurs to Clara Dawes in regard to Paul in *Sons and Lovers*). People who are not just in search of sexual relief (as on some occasions Paul Morel is) choose their sexual partners for attributes not all of which can be traced back to sex, or at least uniquely and directly to sex; and some of them can be very fastidious about it, as Lawrence himself appears to have been. Making every aspect of love dependent on sex leads to the conflation of the two terms, and the elimination from a relationship of much that makes it most human and (in the more favourable cases) delightful. There is a whole area of interest here which had greatly preoccupied novelists before Lawrence and which he largely ignores. However much talk of love there may be in his writing, there are few descriptions of what being in love feels like, and the behaviour it induces in lovers, despite the relatively frequent appearance of the word in his titles.

Baynes makes clear that Lawrence's unconvincing logic in no way diminished the attraction she felt for him and that, although they did not sleep together on the spot, nor indeed the next day, it was on the day after, when he had come for Sunday lunch, that they sat together holding hands until it was dark. 'And so to bed', is how she ends her account.[10] This is all she says about the actual sex but if on sleeping with Lawrence she had found him impotent, or in some other way deeply unsatisfactory, she would presumably either have said so, in these notes recorded only for herself, or not said anything at all. The whole manner and tone of what she records is of someone wanting to remember a pleasant experience.

Whether it was a pleasant experience for Lawrence is not known since the letters he later wrote to Baynes, while affectionate, make no reference to their having been anything more than friends. This is understandable given that Frieda was her friend also and oversaw the letters her husband wrote to her, sometimes adding to them. It is understandable, that is, on the assumption Lawrence kept what had happened secret. Without the letters, the only clue to his feelings is the very complicated one of the poems he wrote while he was with Baynes. Some of these certainly have a voluptuous feel, the one about figs, which figures so prominently in Ken Russell's film of *Women in Love*, being a good example; but this is also the period of the tortoise series. Some of Lawrence's early verse is, as I have suggested, disfigured by his anthropomorphism but in *Birds, Beasts and Flowers* he is able to stand further away from objects in Nature and observe them more closely. This is what he does in the six poems about tortoises, describing those curious creatures with a specificity and warm appreciation which is unparalleled even if anyone who uses human ideas and language to convey an impression of the non-human is inevitably and inescapably anthropomorphic to some extent.

What Lawrence admires in the tiny baby tortoise he begins by introducing is the impression it gives of independence, the quality of being 'alone, with no sense of being alone'. It appears to have no sense of family connection so that 'It is no use my saying to him in an emotional voice: 'This is your Mother, she laid you when you were an egg'. Despite its size the baby tortoise strikes him as a bold adventurer – 'Whither away, small bird?' – yet it bears on its back markings which form the cross that it will eventually have to carry, the Schopenhaurean urge to reproduce seen here in a much less optimistic form than the god Lawrence had referred to in his conversation with Baynes. Switching his attention from the baby tortoise to its parents, he notes how the spear is now through the side of the adult male tortoise who is 'Doomed, in the long crucifixion of desire, to seek his consummation beyond himself', and doomed also therefore to make 'an intolerable fool of himself'. Lawrence describes how the male scuttles after the much larger female pulling at her leg with his beak-like mouth, and then makes a discovery about these strange creatures which surprises him. He had assumed that they were dumb but finds, in the last poem of the six called 'Tortoise Shout', that this is not the case:

Crucifixion.
Male tortoise, cleaving behind the hovel-wall of that dense
    female,
Mounted and tense, spread-eagle, out-reaching out of the
    shell
In tortoise nakedness,
Long neck, and long vulnerable limbs extruded,
    spread-eagle over her house roof,
And the deep, secret, all-penetrating tail curved beneath
    her walls,
Reaching and gripping tense, more reaching anguish in
    uttermost tension
Till suddenly, in the spasm of coition, tupping like a
    jerking leap, and oh!
Opening its clenched face from his outstretched neck
And giving that fragile yell, that scream,
Super-audible,
From his pink, cleft, old-man's mouth, …[11]

'Tortoise Shout' is not one of the poems which Baynes marked in her copy of *Birds, Beasts and Flowers* as having been written while Lawrence was with her but he himself identifies it as belonging to that period.[12] What it expresses may have had nothing at all to do with the brief moment of intimacy they had together, but faint echoes of the horror it conveys can certainly be heard in some of his descriptions of sexual intercourse in the novels, and the idea of sex as a crucifixion is one that reaches at least as far back as 'Last Words to Miriam', although there it is the female and not the male who is the victim.

COMEDY

Between finishing *The Lost Girl* and writing the tortoise poems Lawrence experimented with describing the relations between men

and women, and more specifically his own with Frieda, in a light-
er fashion. In November 1920 he began a novel called *Mr. Noon*,
named after its protagonist, the first part of which looks back to the
misfortunes which overtook his friend, George Neville, when he
was responsible for a girl friend becoming pregnant. At the time,
the news of this event troubled Lawrence a great deal. Jessie Chambers describes how he arrived at the farm house where she lived
with her parents 'white and upset' having heard only that morning
from his mother that Neville had 'got a girl into trouble': 'He was
very distressed. His mother had said how terrible might be the consequences of only five minutes' self forgetfulness'. Jessie adds that
he then startled her by bursting out vehemently 'Thank God ...I've
been saved from that ... so far'.[13] Fourteen years later he felt able
to treat the matter in a comic vein and give a brilliant account of
the courtship rituals that obtained in his adolescence and youth, in
particular the 'spooning' which took place between young couples,
and the unwritten rules, which Neville had clearly broken, that determined, in the words of the title of a once popular David Lodge
novel, how far you could go. But the tone is uncertain, hovering
uneasily between affectionate concern for the difficulties of young
people from his own, pre-war social milieu, and superior, enlightened amusement at those who, with contraception available, fail to
realise that when two young people are strongly attracted to each
other, the only decent thing is that they should sleep together.

In Part Two of this novel there is a complete change of tack with
Gilbert Noon no longer based on Neville but on Lawrence himself.
Before the work breaks off, never to be finished or published in its
author's life-time, there has been a revealing account of Lawrence's
first months of living on the continent with Frieda (called here Johanna), not entirely reliable from a biographical point of view but
offering a valuable emotional record, close to that in *Look! We Have
Come Through!* although in a quite different vein.

Johanna only happens to meet Noon because she has been
fascinated by a Japanese man who has been squeezing her knees

between his on the train so that she misses getting off at the right station. When she seeks refuge in her brother-in-law's flat, Noon is the only person there and she quickly regales him with an account of her husband who, early in their marriage, fell on his knees and called her his 'snowflower'. She describes the lovers she has had since marrying, chief among whom has been Eberhard, a psycho-analyst 'more brilliant than Freud' who has made her believe in 'the sacredness of love', and that there can't be love without sex: 'Eberhard taught me that. And it is so true. Love *is* sex'. In a demonstration that Johanna is not slow to practise what she preaches, she invites Noon into her bed at the conclusion of this first meeting.[14]

As the relationship develops Johanna loosens up her new English partner so that, at one moment, they dance together naked in their German flat. Sex again is described as a rebirth and there is the familiar oscillation between love and hate which, as the hate predominates, leads Johanna to demand to sleep in a separate bed, as Anna does in *The Rainbow*. Whenever she grows away from Noon, he is like Will Brangwen in being forced to recognise and resent his emotional dependence: 'It is a terrible thing to realise that our soul's sanity and integrity depends upon the adjustment of another individual to ourself: that if this individual, wantonly or by urgency break the adjustment and depart, the soul must bleed to death, not whole, and not quite sane.'[15] What, however, seems to receive more emphasis and prominence in *Mr. Noon* than it does in previous texts is the hero's occasional need to escape from women, and his own woman in particular, into a world of men. When, for instance, some soldiers pass by:

He forgot the woman at his side – and love, and happiness. And his heart burned to be with the men, the strange, dark, heavy soldiery, so young and strong with life, reckless and sensual. He wanted it – he wanted it – and not only life with a woman. The thrill of soldiery went heavily through his blood: the glamour of the dark, positive fighting spirit.[16]

These feelings are certainly present in *Look!* yet it seems as if, after eight years of living with Frieda, Lawrence has given them more importance than they had when he first met her.

Much of what is specifically new in *Mr. Noon* can partly be attributed to the jocular framework in which Lawrence now chose to tell his story. Almost immediately after his death his former friend, Middleton Murry, produced a biography (*Son of Woman*) in which he claimed that, largely because of the difficulties he had experienced with his mother, Lawrence was never able to satisfy a woman.[17] As if in anticipation of this, there is a moment in *Mr. Noon* when Johanna says: 'Do you know, I was rather frightened that you weren't a good lover. But it isn't every man who can love a woman three times in a quarter of an hour – *so well* – is it –?' This is followed by one of the direct addresses from the author all too characteristic of the novel:

> And yes, gentle reader – I hope the sterner sex has left off reading before now, so that I may address you alone – Yes, gentle reader, and at what better price can a woman take a man for good? A woman may have the most marvellous pure esteem for a man: but *is* that any reason why she should sleep with him? She may feel her soul carried away to mid-heaven by him: but *does* it therefore follow that she should unfasten her garters? ... I can see absolutely no sounder ground for a permanent marriage than Johanna's – three times in a quarter of an hour, and *so well*. Then you know what you're in for.[18]

This is a much attenuated example of a tone which makes some parts of *Mr. Noon* hard to read: the adoption of a narrative persona which would be Fieldingesque were it not so distinctly lacking in geniality, and simultaneously hostile and defensive. Here it only leaves the reader in some doubt about whether to take Lawrence's claim seriously, although when she read *Son of Woman* Frieda vehemently denied that Lawrence had been anything other than sexually satisfactory in their early days together. Later on in *Mr. Noon*, however, we are told explicitly that Gilbert rather lacked expertise as a lover and that therefore he 'was no wonderful experience for Johanna, though she was a wonderful experience to him'. This bald statement then very surprisingly continues with, 'To tell the truth, Johanna had had far more sensual satisfaction out of her husband'.[19]

Lawrence may have stopped writing *Mr. Noon* because he realised it had become unpublishable or found the comic mode difficult to sustain, given his subject matter. It may have been also that, having just dramatised the moment during his and Frieda's walk from Germany into Italy in 1912, when she told him that she had slept with David Garnett's friend Hobson, he found the material becoming too painful or difficult. The text as a whole is warmly supportive of Johanna's free-and-easy attitude to sex but that is in contradiction with Noon's need for commitment from her, as it was with Lawrence's belief in marriage as a permanent bond (only temporarily and perhaps regretfully suspended in the case of Rosalind Baynes). Whatever the reasons, it is not, from a literary point of view, a success, but that is certainly not true of a novella he wrote a little later about love, although love much more in the Stendhalian sense than his own. Ortega y Gasset complained that in *De l'amour* the lover creates a false image of the beloved, yet for Stendhal this was a large part of the point and he believed that the intense imaginative life an unrequited lover enjoys meant that Goethe's Werther was a more enviable figure than Don Giovanni.[20] Whether or not this is true for the lover, Lawrence was more concerned with what it felt like to be on the receiving end of such love. In a late poem called 'Image-making love', he wrote:

Always
in the eyes of those who loved me
I have seen at last the image of him they loved
and took for me
mistook for me.

And always
it was a simulacrum, something
like me, and like a gibe at me.[21]

The novella he wrote in 1921 on this theme successfully maintains a light comic tone throughout. It is called 'The Captain's Doll' and concerns the relationship a Scottish army officer has formed with a deracinated bohemian countess who is living in the German town where he is stationed after the war. Hannele is this countess's name and she is something of an artist. As what she thinks of as a tribute to her lover, she has made a doll of him which is amazingly life-like ('You've got me', is the subject's own verdict). So true to life is it that when the Captain's bossy wife arrives from England to reclaim her husband, she immediately knows, on seeing the doll, that whoever made it must have slept with him. Lawrence's talent for sophisticated social comedy is very much under-estimated and the scene in which Hannele and the Captain's wife fight for possession of the doll has a Wildean feel which helps avoid any too obvious symbolic significance. After the wife's supposedly accidental death, the two lovers are separated for a while and Hannele sells her doll. This means that when the Captain comes to another German-speaking town, hoping to persuade her to marry him rather than the Austrian official to whom she had become engaged, he is humiliated to discover that the purchaser was a surrealist painter who has depicted the doll in one of his canvasses, alongside 'two sunflowers in a glass jar, and a poached egg on toast'. Having bought the painting, he suggests to Hannele that there should be for them a variation on the traditional marriage vows which reads 'honour, obedience and the proper physical feelings', and he justifies the crucial omission of 'love' by pointing out 'when … we were supposed to be in love with one another, you made that doll of me'. Honour and obedience are hard for an independent woman like Hannele to swallow but, in the final action, she asks the Captain to give her the painting so that she can destroy it.[22] Birkin is suspicious of Ursula's offer of love in *Women in Love* because it might be an excuse for enveloping him into herself, as a mother might her baby; or because, in the words Lawrence used to Rosalind Baynes, it might prove 'that most indecent kind of egotism and self-spreading'. Hepburn wants to point out that he is a person in his own right and not just someone on whom Hannele can project her own preferred image. His reference to sex as 'the proper physical feelings' is probably the least dramatic in the whole of Lawrence's *oeuvre*. For a brief moment, it is as if sexual intercourse were not something of immense significance but just part and parcel of normal married life.

MAGNUS

The Captain's Doll was written while Lawrence and Frieda were in Zell-am-See in Austria. Between leaving England as soon as they were able in 1919 and setting out for the New World at the beginning of 1922, they moved around Western Europe a good deal. Lawrence's own first destination had been Florence (while Frieda was in Germany) so that his brief affair with Rosalind Baynes was not on his first visit to that city. He had gone there initially because in London he had got to know the writer Norman Douglas whose preference for young boys (over his wife) meant that there were legal barriers to his staying in England, and that he was obliged to live abroad. Douglas was at the centre of a circle of expatriate writers and artists in Florence which included some who were entirely homosexual, like Reggie Turner, a minor novelist who had been a loyal friend to Wilde in his final years, and others who, like Douglas himself, had tried marriage but decided they preferred sexual relations with members of their own sex. One of these latter was Maurice Magnus, an American-born impresario (he had once been the manager of Isadora Duncan) and a journalist.

When Lawrence had first been made properly aware of Keynes's active homosexuality in Cambridge, he had been horrified; but he was at ease in this Florence group, whether or not Frieda was there with him. He gives a lively account of Douglas's risqué conversation in *Aaron's Rod*, the last novel he published before leaving Europe (although it in fact appeared when he was already on the boat to Australia); and he used Magnus as a model for the dapper, camp individual whom Alvina's father employs to manage his venture into theatre and silent cinema in *The Lost Girl*. Mr. May is the name he gives to this character and his treatment includes a good deal of malice. Yet he was attracted to Magnus, or at least intrigued by him. A Roman Catholic, Magnus was friendly with the monks in the then famous monastery at Monte Casino, and invited Lawrence to visit him there. When he did this in February 1920 he was living in Capri and the journey took eleven hours. He then only stayed a couple of nights and one whole day, so there must have been something about Magnus which he liked for him to take the trouble. Later that year however, when he was settled in Taormina with Frieda, he was not pleased to find an anxious Magnus suddenly turning up at his door, on the run from the police. Always irresponsible about money, and with expensive tastes, he had signed a few checks that had bounced. It might well be that he had gone to Monte Cassino to hide from the consequences of his actions, but the authorities had tracked him down there and he had been obliged to make a precipitous retreat down into Sicily. Much to Frieda's disgust, Lawrence lent him some money from their own modest funds and Magnus then moved to Malta where he hoped to be beyond Italian police jurisdiction. This happened to be at the same time as Lawrence himself took a trip there, accompanied by Frieda and Mary Cannan (an old friend). While he was in Malta, he spent some time with Magnus who reported back to Norman

Douglas the upshot of what must have been quite intimate conversations. Lawrence, he claimed,

> is looking for bi-sexual types for *himself*. Spoke of his innocence when he wrote 'Twilight' and 'Il Duro'. Evidently innocent no longer. Didn't like Malta because he thought that the religion or something prevented their sexual expression! I didn't elucidate him as I could have done even after a few days stay! He revels in all that is just not within his reach. He wants it to be within his reach. Arrived too late – regrets it. Never speaks of it unless bored to tears by women as here by Mrs. Cannan and his wife.[23]

Since this corresponds with much of what we know about Lawrence, it is hard to dismiss as entirely malicious gossip. The key to what Magnus says seems to be Lawrence's regret at his former ignorance of his sexual nature, at his innocence. He is now 'innocent no longer', although Magnus immediately casts doubt on that claim by suggesting that, in spite of whatever restrictions the Church imposed in Malta, he himself has been able to identify the island's gay scene in only a few days. 'Il Duro' is the vine grafter who features in Lawrence's travel book, *Twilight in Italy*. Between him and its author there appears to have been a good deal of attraction, and he is described in *Twilight* as having decided to give up on women.[24] The implication is that Lawrence felt he was too innocent at the time he met il Duro to recognise a fellow bisexual, and do something about it. Now (according to Magnus) he regrets that it is all too late.

Magnus was over-optimistic in believing his financial difficulties would not catch up with him in Malta, and when they did he chose to commit suicide rather than go to prison or carry on running. This was a shock to Lawrence who felt some responsibility and perhaps guilt, in part because there had been a point at which he had refused to lend Magnus any more money, but chiefly on

account of two Maltese who had been introduced to him by Lawrence and from whom Magnus had borrowed considerably. He felt
that by writing an introduction to a memoir Magnus had left behind about the time he had spent in the French Foreign Legion, he
could get this text into print and make enough money to reimburse
the Maltese. He was later to say that this introduction was the best
piece of writing ('as writing') he had ever done,[25] and certainly it
offers a vivid and entertaining portrait of Magnus, with his dandi-
fied appearance, fussing around Douglas and agreeing with him
that the best time to spend money was when you did not happen
to have any. Lawrence had clearly not met such a mixture of the
fastidious and brash before and was fascinated by it. He records his
surprise at Magnus at one moment saying to him at table: 'How
lovely your hair is – such a lovely colour! What do you dye it with?',
and adds that he felt he was not believed when he explained that
whatever colour his hair had (mousey with a reddish tinge) was
natural.[26]

That a man who displayed so many effeminate mannerisms
should possess the underlying toughness which enabled him to
survive the near-barbarism of life in the Foreign Legion was astonishing to Lawrence and filled him with admiration. But when he
came to consider Magnus's references to the sexual mores he found
there, the tone of passages which were omitted when his introduction was published became severe and condemnatory. This was not
because the degree to which homosexuality was rife in the Legion
surprised him. 'Everyone knows that a natural activity in the life of
real soldier is drinking prostitution and homosexuality', Lawrence
had written in that part of 'The Crown' which deals with same-
sex desire.[27] What disgusted him was the indignant tone Magnus
himself adopted when he described how couples would form in
the Legion in which the active, stronger partner would carry the
pack of the *girant*, a word which Magnus mistakenly assumed was
French slang for a passive homosexual.

They were so terribly *indecent,* the Legionaries. No doubt, dear Maurice. 'It doesn't matter *what* you do, it's the *way you do it!*'. – That was one of his favourite clap-traps. I quite agree, my dear. It *is* the way you do it. You spy out a comely looking individual, of the 'lower classes', you invite him to smokes and drinks – and afterwards you *pay* him – *Alles in Ehren*! –all nice in honor, don't you know! – The way you do it! – Oh yes, money will cover multitudes upon multitudes of sins … Just *look* at the degraded Legionary, carrying the pack of his *girant* and doing his chores for him! Wouldn't twenty francs have been *so* much more decent in every way![28]

Lawrence obviously feels it would not have been more decent, and he is angry at the way Magnus exploited other people's feelings: 'He came up so winsomely to appeal for affection. He took the affection and paid back twenty francs', or (in Lawrence's own case), he took the affection and asked to borrow money. As for the 'poor devils of legionaries. They had their blood passions and carried them defiantly, flagrantly, to depravity'. What Lawrence says distresses him about the Legion is the sense of 'so much genuine creative blood-passion being self-destroyed'. He probably means by this that, in normal circumstances, the Legionaries would be heterosexual but his more important point is that 'the blood passions are sacred', whatever their orientation, and that they are worth much more than the kind of 'mind or spirit or uplift' in which Magnus believed.[29] His protest is against a certain kind of homosexual lifestyle he had had the opportunity to observe in Magnus, and no doubt in other members of the Douglas group, and not the homosexuality itself.

Aaron's Rod

The eponymous hero of *Aaron's Rod* is a working man who plays the flute very well and, at the beginning of the novel, is shown walking out on his wife Lottie and their children. This means that Lawrence can then indulge in a satirical account of what it feels like to be a working-class artist suddenly thrown into a world of middle-class intellectuals. Since the novel was begun in 1917, there are portraits here of writers Lawrence had met during the war, Richard Aldington, for example, or Hilda Doolittle, who was always known as H.D.; but by then moving the action to Florence, he was able to incorporate figures in the Douglas circle, including Magnus and 'wicked uncle Norman' himself.

The most important of the acquaintances Aaron makes in his new life is Rawdon Lilly, who is married to a Norwegian called Tanny and functions as a Lawrentian alter ego. Lilly is more than sympathetic when this former checkweighman at a local mine tries to explain quite why he has left his wife, and complains of the hold women have over men. For him, all women want of a man is to father their children, to which Lilly adds that '*they* must be loved, at any price! ... And if you just don't want to love them – and tell them so – what a crime'. A little later it is Lilly who says, 'You learn to be quite alone – and possess your own soul in isolation – and at the same time, to be perfectly *with* someone else – that's all I ask'.[30] This is all that Birkin asked too but the 'at the same time' makes it a difficult trick to bring off. Being simultaneously at one and separate was expressed for Birkin by the concept of stellar polarity. When Aaron is trying to ponder the enigma of love and sex, he finds a different image:

> Love too. But there also, taking one's way alone, happily alone in all the wonders of communion, swept up on the winds, but never swept away from one's very self. Two eagles in mid-air, maybe, like Whitman's 'Dalliance of

Eagles'. Two eagles in mid-air, grappling, whirling, coming to their intensification of love-oneness there in mid-air. In mid-air the love consummation. But all the time each lifted on its own wings: each bearing itself up on its own wings at every moment of the mid-air love consummation. That is the splendid love-way.[31]

'The Dalliance of Eagles' is one of Whitman's best short poems but, as an image of love or love-making, it turns out to be, on the most cursory examination, entirely different from Birkin's stellar polarity. In the latter, for example, the two stars are part of the same system of forces and therefore remain unified and in a way dependent on each other even while apart. After their mid-air copulation, on the other hand, the two eagles' separation is conclusive:

> A motionless still balance in the air, then parting, talons
>   loosing,
> Upward again on slow-firm pinions slanting, their
>   separate and diverse flight,
> She hers, he his, pursuing.[32]

Rather than being a formula for a simultaneous being together and apart, 'separate and diverse' suggests free love or casual sex, after which there is no need for further communion.

Because it was begun just after the completion of *Women in Love, Aaron's Rod* is full of similar ideas as that novel, but the tone is entirely different. An indication of this is that at one point the narrator says 'When a man writes a letter to himself, it is a pity to post it to someone else. Perhaps the same is true of a book'.[33] In the early part, Aaron has a brief fling with a member of a London literary and artistic set called Josephine Ford. That so upsets him that it is credited with paving the way to a bad bout of influenza. Having collapsed in the street he finds himself being looked after by Lilly, whose wife has gone to visit her relatives abroad. Since one of his symptoms is constipation, Lilly adopts the unusual method of uncovering 'the blond lower body of his patient' and massaging it with camphorated oil: 'He rubbed every speck of the man's lower body – the abdomen, the buttocks, the thighs and knees, down to the feet'. He is pleased that, as a result of this treatment, he is able to see a 'spark come back into the sick eyes'.[34] Whatever its medicinal value, this ritual appears to be not so very far removed from the bathing scene in *The White Peacock*, and the naked wrestling in *Women in Love*, in that it represents a strange form of male bonding and an alternative to the threat constituted by relations with women, whether they be girl friends, wives or mistresses. That is confirmed when, very shortly afterwards, Lilly and Aaron engage in that conversation about women only wanting men so that they can have children, or demanding to be loved, from which I have already quoted. But despite what he says in the unpublished Whitman essay, Lawrence offers no suggestion that the intimacy Lilly and Aaron establish could ever eventuate in direct sexual activity of some kind. What is however new in this scene is Lilly's consciousness of his superiority over Aaron, and his feeling that, if they are to have a relationship, he would like that superiority acknowledged. That is to say that, having looked deeper into relations between men and discovered the same power struggle that troubled him in his dealings with women, Lawrence appears to have begun to feel that the only solution was for one party to assert superiority and persuade the other to accept it, for after all, as he increasingly insisted, the Christian and democratic emphasis on all men being equal flew in the face of observable fact.

Forgetful of the lessons his affair with Josephine Ford might have taught him – 'I gave into her', he says, '– and afterwards I cried, and thought of (my wife) and the children'[35] – Aaron stumbles into another when he is in Florence, this time with an American woman married to an Italian Marchese. But this turns out to be no happier in its consequences than his first and, on one occasion, he is filled with revulsion once the sex is over:

> But when he was dressed and bent over her to say goodbye, she put her arms round him, that seem such frail and child- ish arms now, yet withal so deadly in power. Her soft arms round his neck, her tangle of hair over his face. And yet, even as he kissed her, he felt her deadly. He wanted to be gone. He wanted to get out of her arms and her clinging and her tangle of hair and her curiosity and her strange and hateful power.[36]

This is hardly what happens after the dalliance of eagles and seems to indicate something much more than post-coital sadness. The problem does not appear to be one of a failure to satisfy his partner since the text makes it clear that, between the late morning and early afternoon of this meeting, sexual intercourse takes place three times. Although this is a less noteworthy example of sexual athleti- cism than Mr. Noon's three times in fifteen minutes, it is important that it occurs in a context where Aaron has become worried about his lack of interest in sex. 'For such a long time', Lawrence writes, '…(Aaron) had wanted nothing, his desire had kept itself back, fast back. For such a long time his desire for woman had withheld itself, hard and resistant'.[37] This is the beginning of a concern with impotence, whether psychological or physiological, which will run through the rest of Lawrence's writing. The 'rod' of the novel's title refers to the flute Aaron plays, but is also phallic. What is suggested is that its flowering is only now occasional. When the affair with the Marchesa comes to an end, another character tells Aaron that he will have to live without his rod for a while, a reference which is not only to the instrument he happens to have lost.

But if anxieties about performance do not explain Aaron's re- vulsion, what can? There is certainly a general suspicion of female power that had been characteristic of Lawrence since *Women in*

Love (if not before), but also perhaps a discomfort, which Aaron mentions from time to time, that he is after all a married man, and which can be related to his creator. Whereas for Frieda extra-marital affairs posed no problem, even the idea of them appears to have presented Lawrence with thorny difficulties of reluctance and guilt, as 'New Eve and Old Adam' had already implied. Apart from these factors however, there are still other difficulties suggested by details in the text. On the first of the three occasions on which Aaron and the Marchesa make love in the scene from which I have quoted, for example, he feels that in her clinging to him she is like a child but one who 'in some deep and essential way mocked him'. When he wakes after a short sleep and they make love again 'his desire had an element of cruelty in it: something rather brutal. He took *his* way with her now, and she had no chance now of the curious opposition, because of the way he took her.'[38] Although the reference here is no where near as clear as it sometimes is elsewhere, it would seem that anal intercourse is once again in play and that for Aaron, as indeed for Lawrence, what it represented was the opportunity for a male exertion of dominance and power. More generally, what these words suggest is that Aaron and the Marchesa are involved in mutual exploitation of each other's bodies. Lawrence is perhaps clearer about his protagonist's eventual attitude to this practice in a cancelled passage from the description of the last occasion on which the two of them make love which appears as an appendix in the Cambridge edition of the novel. There Aaron freely admits that, as far as exploitation goes, he is no better than the Marchesa but that nevertheless 'a certain deep dislike of her now began to creep into him':

> Nothing is more offensive to any wholesome individual, man or woman, than to feel he or she is appropriated and made to serve the other person's gratification or convenience. No wholesome person can bear to be made use of. And if it be a case of: 'I'll let you make use of me, if you'll

let me make use of you', this, indeed, is a bargain, but it is a bargain one always regrets, whilst one remains oneself, and whole. A bargain one not only regrets, but resents and deeply begrudges.[39]

When in *The Rainbow* Will and Anna Brangwen reach a stage in their sex life when they are content to make the most of each other's bodies, Lawrence gives little indication of what would or could follow on from there. Here, his answer seems to be resentment and deep dislike although whereas he is convincing about Aaron's feelings of being used, he tells us too little about the Marchesa to persuade us that, in sexual terms, she is in fact an instinctive 'user' of other people. But whether readers ought to think of her in that way or not, the more general problem is one Lawrence had struggled with before. Once sexual intercourse had performed one or other of the various functions with which he was willing to credit it, what alternative was there to the descent into mutual exploitation and what he calls sensationalism? If there is no alternative in his scheme of things, then it is hardly a surprise that the sexual contact which had once promised so much – relief, rebirth, escape from the enclosure of the self, communication with unknown powers – was now often something rather more than a disappointment.

CHAPTER FOUR:
NEW WORLD BUT NOT SO NEW THOUGHTS

KANGAROO

When the Lawrences set out for the United States, they went the long way round, sailing first to what was at that time Ceylon, and then to Australia. Their stay in Ceylon was not a success but they remained in Australia for three months, long enough for Lawrence to write a novel there. *Kangaroo*, as this novel is appropriately called, is like *Aaron's Rod* in being another of what he liked to call thought adventures, that is to say it makes use of a fictional form to work out ideas which were troubling him. Yet as far as love and sex are concerned, it represents variations on what are very much the same themes. The story is told through a travelling English writer called Richard Lovatt Somers (the initials RLS recall another writer who explored the southern hemisphere and was tubercular), and his German wife Harriett. Together they form a couple more instantly recognisable as the Lawrences than any other in his fiction.

The relation of these two characters receives a good deal of attention throughout the novel but the chapter which is focussed exclusively on them is entitled 'Harriett and Lovatt at Sea in Marriage'. What it suggests is that their marriage is at a crossroads with Harriett still insisting that their hymeneal bark should fly the flag of 'perfect love' even when, according to Lovatt, perfect love is a fiasco 'ninety-nine times out of a hundred'. In his view, their real choice is between a drift into companionship and her acceptance of him as her lord and master, and his preference for this second option is indicated when he says that, after all, 'you can't have two masters of one ship: neither can you have a ship without a master'. He wants to replace the tattered ensign of perfect love with one which represents a phoenix, and imagines himself as this mythical bird rising from the nest which is his wife. 'A forward-seeking male', he would like her to 'believe in his adventure and deliver herself over to it' so that they can sail together into 'unchartered seas'. But she is sceptical of his qualifications for mastership and always quick to remind him of how dependent he is on her and on women in general: '"Without *me* you'd be nowhere, you'd be nothing, you'd not be *that*" – and she snapped her fingers under his nose, a movement he particularly disliked'. The dilemma is one which by this stage Lawrence is willing to treat with wry resignation and some humour. Harriett had no desire to be 'a comfortable nest for his impertinence', he writes, nor a domestic slave like Mrs. Gladstone who, when a female friend was lamenting the state of Ireland and comforting herself with the thought that there is after all 'One above', replied that this was quite true and her husband was upstairs changing his socks.[1]

This ability to treat what is normally for Lawrence the intensely serious matter of his relationship with Frieda with ironic and sometimes comic distance had already been evident in a book he had published not long before leaving Europe. *Sea and Sardinia* is the record of a fortnight's trip the Lawrences took to that island in 1921. Written in the form of a diary that manages to give the impression of having been composed on the spot, this short book has an engaging quality which has made it the preferred choice of most of those who are asked to suggest one single text as an introduction to Lawrence, and part of its appeal comes from the way the more everyday nature of marriage is presented. In one early scene, for example, the Lawrences have arrived in Palermo where they are to take the boat for Cagliari. As they mingle with the crowds in one of Palermo's shopping streets, Lawrence is conscious that together they must look like a 'travelling menagerie' since, for economy's sake, he has on his back a big brown knapsack while Frieda is carrying their 'kitchenino', a basket full of implements for making impromptu snacks. This is not how tourists who are immediately recognisable as coming from the north usually travel. 'Suddenly', he writes, 'I am aware of the q-b darting past me like a storm'. Frieda has spotted three young local girls laughing at their appearance and begins abusing them in her 'sledge-hammer Italian' only to incur 'more than sledge-hammer retaliation'. Feeling that he is called upon to say 'something in the manly line', Lawrence intervenes with 'Beastly Palermo bad manners' and throws out a nonchalant 'Ignoranti … in a tone of dismissal'.[2] The incident shows him and Frieda united against the world and calling his wife the 'q-b' – which is short for 'queen bee' (what Birkin had already called Ursula in *Women in Love*)[3] – is an illustration of the way a married couple can grow into humorous acceptance of each other's foibles. It was a certain aristocratic *hauteur*, related to her privileged German background, which caused Lawrence to think of Frieda as a queen bee although, in fact, her casual assumptions of superiority came with qualities which, as details in his portraits of Ursula make clear, he was inclined to admire.

There are recognisable signs of adaptation and compromise in what we glimpse of marriage in both the 'Harriett and Lovatt at Sea' chapter of *Kangaroo* and *Sea and Sardinia*, and even of that 'true friendship and companionship' which Lawrence so distrusts as a road married people can take (for Lovatt, it would make his union with his wife too much like a 'limited liability Company').[4] Companionship in marriage could also be described as love and *Kangaroo* is the only text by him where there is a possible illustration of how this might translate into sex. The Somerses have returned to their house by the sea along the New South Wales coast. It is raining when they arrive but he takes off his clothes, runs in the sea and, after standing under the shower in the 'little wash-place … to wash off the sticky strong Pacific', makes love to Harriet:

To the end she was more wondering than anything. But when it was the end, and the night was falling outside, she laughed and said to him:

'That was done in style. That was *chic*. Straight from the sea, like another creature'.

Style and *chic* seemed to him somewhat ill suited to the occasion, but he brought her a bowl of warm water and went and made the tea.[5]

This has the air of pleasant, uncomplicated sex between two people who have been married for a long time (however much some readers might speculate about the bowl of warm water). Usually in Lawrence sexual intercourse is a test, ordeal, or possible transfiguration; but here it is no more than what married people do from time to time. There is an air of what one might risk calling normality about it, which perhaps relates to the way that the responsibility for its characterisation falls to Harriet rather than her husband.

The major interest of *Kangaroo* does not however lie in the marriage of the Somerses. Shortly after their arrival in Sydney, they find themselves living next door to the Calcotts. Jack Calcott is involved with a right-wing political movement of ex-servicemen for which he tries to recruit Somers, offering him at the same time a distinctively local version of the *Blutbrüdershaft* which, at one moment in *Women in Love*, Birkin has sought from Gerald.[6] What makes it local is that it plays on the traditional importance in Australia of a man's *mate*. The marriage of the Calcotts is an 'open' one and a situation arises where his wife Victoria appears to be offering herself to Somers. Attracted as he is, Somers wonders 'Why not know them all, all the great moments of the gods, from the major moment with Hera to the swift short moments of Io or Leda or Ganymede? Should not a man know the whole range?' But in the end he finds himself too 'stubbornly puritanical' to avail himself of the opportunity being offered.[7] The inclusion of Ganymede in this list is striking. The appeals Jack has made to him have a homoerotic tinge, very much in the mode of Whitman's love of comrades; but far more than a tinge is involved when Somers is introduced by Jack to Ben Cooley, the charismatic Jewish lawyer who leads the movement to which Jack belongs, and who is known as Kangaroo.

Cooley is an advocate of what for Lawrence is a Christian-derived concept of love, the same which, in its social aspects, is analysed so shrewdly in the description in *Women in Love* of the efforts made by Gerald's father to run his coal-mine on Christian principles. (The miners turn out to resent more the relationships which result from these than they do the consequences of Gerald's later establishment of a simple cash nexus between him and them.)[8] Physically attracted though Somers is to Cooley, who seems to him sometimes repulsive but also on occasions attractive so that 'even his body had become beautiful', he is wary of the more personal aspects of Cooley's love, and not so certain of his politics either.[9] A rival appeal comes from Willie Struthers, a Marxist trade unionist who is aware of Somers's working-class background, has also read pieces he has written (when these are described, they turn out to be essays Lawrence himself had published), and wants to recruit him for the political Left rather than the Right. Once he learns of this, Cooley regards it as an act of emotional as well as political betrayal and makes a determined effort to win Somers over:

> Suddenly, with a great massive movement, Kangaroo caught the other man to his breast.
>
> 'Don't Lovatt', he said, in a much moved voice, pressing the slight body of the lesser man against his own big breast and body. 'Don't', he said, with a convulsive tightening of the arm.
>
> Somers, squeezed so that he could hardly breathe, kept his face from Kangaroo's jacket and managed to ejaculate:
>
> 'All right. Let me go and I won't'.
>
> 'Don't thwart me', pleaded Kangaroo 'Don't – or I shall be forced to break all connexion with you, and I love you

so. I love you so. Don't be perverse and put yourself against me'.[10]

But after much havering, reject Cooley is precisely what Somers does just as he has also rejected Jack Calcott and Struthers.

An interesting feature of all three of the advances made by other men to Somers in this novel is that he is quite explicitly cast in a female role. Although this was also true of the narrator in the bathing scene of *The White Peacock*, Birkin in *Women in Love*'s naked wrestling, and Lilly in the oil-rubbing episode in *Aaron's Rod*, both of whom are author surrogates (and the characters readers are asked to identify with), do not have anything particularly female about them, unless ministering to the sick is to be regarded as exclusively woman's work. But when Somers first arrives in Australia he becomes conscious of how small he is in comparison with most of the population and especially, because it is hot enough to wear shorts or people spend a good deal of time on the beach, how thin his legs are in comparison with theirs. Jack's suggestion is that he should become the 'queen bee' of their hive,[11] which is ironic given what Lawrence liked to call Frieda, and there are repeated references to Somers as being like a woman, a she-man. It may be that being cast so firmly in a female role, and the passivity this traditionally implies, influences how Somers finally responds to Jack, Struthers and Cooley; but his refusal of what Birkin above all had been seeking is nevertheless something of a watershed, not only in this novel but in Lawrence's work as a whole:

> He had all his life had this craving for an absolute friend, a David to his Jonathan, Pylades to his Orestes: a blood brother. All his life he had secretly grieved over his friendlessness. And now at last, when it really offered – and it had offered twice before, since he had left Europe – he didn't want it, and he realised in his innermost soul that he had never wanted it.

Yet he wanted *some* living fellowship with other men: as it was he was just isolated. Maybe a living fellowship! – but not affection, not love, not comradeship. Not mates and equality and mingling. Not blood brotherhood. None of that.[12]

Scenes of male bonding do not disappear from Lawrence's fiction from this moment on, but they do change in character and suggest that his bi-sexuality became much less of an issue for him as he grew older.[13]

With his relationship with Harriet not especially satisfactory, and all those with men a failure, Somers is driven back in *Kangaroo* to Nature. In *Women in Love*, there is a strange scene where, after an exasperated Hermione has hit Birkin over the head with a ball of lapis lazuli, he retreats to the countryside, takes off all his clothes, and rolls around in the wet vegetation. Moving through a clump of young fir trees, 'soft sharp boughs beat upon him … threw cold showers of drops on his belly, and beat his loins with their clusters of soft-sharp needles'. For Birkin to lie down and 'roll in the sticky, cool young hyacinths', Lawrence writes, was 'soft and more delicate and more beautiful than the touch of a woman'.[14] What is apparent there is that the narcissism evident in some of his early writing has developed into a powerful and bizarre form of what a sceptic would call auto-eroticism. Something similar to Birkin's sensual communing with the natural world occurs near the very end of *Kangaroo* when, under a full moon, Somers goes for a walk on the beach, his only company a nearby group of wild ponies. He is described as 'rocking with the radium-urgent passion of the night'; and the next phrase ('the huge, desirous swing, the call, clamour, the low hiss of retreat') suggests his complete identification with the waves coming in:

The call, call! And the answerer. Where was his answerer? There was no living answerer. No dark-bodied, warm

bodied answerer. He knew that when he had spoken a
word to the night-half-hidden ponies with their fluffy legs.
No animate answer this time. The radium-rocking, wave-
knocking night his call and his answer both. This God
without feet or knees or face. This sluicing, knocking, urg-
ing night, heaving like a woman with unspeakable desire,
but no woman, no thighs or breast, no body. The moon,
the concave mother-of-pearl of night, the great radium
swinging, and his little self. The call and the answer, without intermediary. Non-human Gods, non-human human
being.[15]

Since the Romantics everyone has been aware that the natural world
can be a consolation in times of emotional distress. But Lawrence
gives to the Wordsworthian expression 'a lover of Nature' meanings
which that poet could have hardly dreamt of. For him, when erotic
satisfaction is denied by other human beings it can be discovered,
or at least sought, in the natural world.

THE PLUMED SERPENT

Aaron's Rod, and *Kangaroo* in particular, are signs of Lawrence's increasing interest in politics, in how the world should be governed
after the cataclysm of World War One. They are the beginnings of
a period in his life when love and sex become of only secondary
interest. This trend continued when he finally arrived in North
America and, after a period in the New Mexican town of Taos,
settled on a ranch nearby which had been given to Frieda by an
American patroness of the arts called Mabel Sterne. While he was
there he made two extended visits to Mexico, separated by a brief
return to Europe in the winter of 1923–4. An indication that the
novel he wrote in Mexico was not, as *Aaron's Rod* and *Kangaroo* had
been, a casual affair, is that on his first visit he wrote a draft which
he entitled *Quetzalcoatl* while, on the second, he extensively revised

this into a much longer text which – to what was no doubt his publisher's relief – he decided to call *The Plumed Serpent*. Both titles refer to a god from the old, pre-Christian Mexican pantheon, the second being a translation into English of the attributes of the first.

Whereas *Kangaroo* offers a critique of existing political schemes, Lawrence attempts in *The Plumed Serpent* to describe, in a meticulous detail which refers chiefly to dress and liturgy, what a theocracy, inspired by the old Aztec religion, would look like. The prime movers of the attempt to install this variety of authoritarian regime in Mexico are two old friends called Ramón Carrasco and Cipriano Viedma who are bound together in what can certainly look like the sort of blood brotherhood Somers had so decisively rejected in *Kangaroo*. In *The Plumed Serpent* there is ceremony by means of which Cipriano is magically supposed to become the living Huitzilopochtli, the Aztec god of war, Ramón having chosen to represent and embody the god of the novel's title, Quetzalcoatl. Lawrence seems to have had more satisfaction from inventing such ceremonies, and composing the hymns which often accompany them, than most readers derive from reading the results. The two men are alone and, among many other physical contacts, Ramón binds his friend fast round the middle with black fur, presses his head against Cipriano's hip, folds his arms round his loins, and closes, with his hands, 'the secret places'.[16] The homoeroticism of this is inescapable, yet there is one important difference from blood brotherhood rituals in the earlier novels. In *Aaron's Rod*, Lilly had struggled and failed to make Aaron accept that their relationship should be imbalanced; but there is no doubt in *The Plumed Serpent* that Cipriano is Ramón's subordinate. Whatever friendship they enjoy is based on the recognition and acceptance of hierarchy, as indeed is the whole political system the two of them want to introduce. Blood brotherhood in the old sense is by contrast associated with a New Testament-derived notion of equality; but Lawrence had come to believe that its message of treating not just close friends but everyone as 'born equal', to echo the American declaration of independence, was an hypocrisy, and one which had, like the Christian socialism of his youth, been exposed by the barbarities of the First World War.

Ramón is unhappily married to a devout Roman Catholic called Carlota and this gives Lawrence the opportunity to enlarge on why the old, indigenous religion needs to be reinstated. She can not understand when her husband refuses to go on being gentle, good and loving while his own view is that 'the world had gone as far as it could go in the good, gentle and loving direction, and anything further in that line meant perversity'. Her own love for Ramón is no longer a spontaneous flow: 'She loved him with the *will*: as the white world now tends to do. She became filled with charity, that cruel kindness.' When later he expands on how his difficulties with Carlota have affected their sex life, he claims that although with a woman a man always wants to let himself go, that is precisely what he should not do.

> It's no good a man ravishing a woman, and it's absolutely no good a woman ravishing a man. … Absurd as it may sound, it is not I who would ravish Carlota. It is she who would ravish me. Strange and absurd and a little shameful, it is true. – Letting oneself go, is either ravishing or being ravished. Oh, if we could only abide by our souls, and meet in the abiding place.[17]

As far as sexual intercourse is concerned, this 'abiding place' proves to be even more mysterious than Birkin's stellar polarity and it would be hard to distinguish between what for Lawrence had been in the past the pleasures and rewards of 'lapsing out' and Ramón's reference here to letting oneself go.

The recipient of Ramón's confidences about his marriage is a forty-year old European called Kate Leslie. She has had children by a first husband, from whom she is divorced, and is now the widow of a second who was an Irish political leader. Kate acts as a sceptical European observer of the schemes of Ramón and Cipriano, with a noticeable lessening of the scepticism between *Quetzalcoatl* and *The Plumed Serpent*. She is attracted to Cipriano but, in the first version of the novel, inhibited by essentially racist doubts about miscegenation. By the time of *The Plumed Serpent* these have disappeared, perhaps because the not very creditable shock which Lawrence and Frieda registered when they first learnt that Mabel Sterne, their hostess in Taos, had actually married her Indian lover (Tony Luhan) had quietened down, and they had come to accept the union.[18]

What attracts Kate to Cipriano is his 'phallic' power. He is a recurrent figure in Lawrence's fiction, the dark stranger who brings sexual regeneration to an etiolated milieu: apart from Ciccio in *The Lost Girl*, a notable forerunner is Count Dionys in *The Ladybird*, one of the novellas which Lawrence wrote before they left Europe.[19] Shortly before crossing the Atlantic a common way he had developed of describing these characters was by reference to the Greek god Pan and, in his account of what Kate begins to feel, sitting side by side with Cipriano in a motor car, Pan continues to make an appearance. What she was recognising in Cipriano, Lawrence writes, was 'the ancient phallic mystery, the ancient god-devil of the male Pan ... He had the old gift of demon-power':

> He would never woo: she saw this. When the power of his blood rose in him, the dark aura streamed from him like a cloud pregnant with power, like thunder, and rose like a whirlwind that rises suddenly in the twilight and raises a great plaint column, swaying and leaning with power, clear between heaven and earth.
>
> Ah! and what a mystery of prone submission, on her part, this huge erection would imply! Submission absolute, like the earth under the sky. Beneath an over-arching absolute.
>
> Ah! what a marriage! How terrible! and how complete![20]

Despite what is possibly an inadvertent and certainly embarrassing reference to a 'huge erection', the language here is only vaguely evocative, as it usually is when Lawrence comes to deal with actual physical contacts between Kate and Cipriano in *The Plumed Serpent*. Yet in exploring the question later of 'prone submission', or 'submission absolute', he is capable of being troublingly specific. The effect of Cipriano's love-making, Lawrence writes, is to make Kate's 'strange, seething feminine will and desire' subside in her:

> She realised, almost with wonder, the death in her of the Aphrodite of the foam: the seething, frictional, ecstatic Aphrodite. By a swift dark instinct, Cipriano drew away from this in her. When, in their love, it came back on her, the seething electric female ecstasy, which knows such spasms of delirium, he recoiled from her. It was what she used to call her 'satisfaction'. She had loved Joachim [her second husband] for this, that again, and again, and again he could give her this orgiastic 'satisfaction', in spasms that made her cry aloud.
>
> But Cipriano would not. By a dark and powerful instinct he drew away from her as soon as this desire arose again in her, for the white ecstasy of frictional satisfaction, the throes of Aphrodite of the foam. She could see that, to him, it was repulsive. He just removed himself, dark and unchangeable, away from her.

Cipriano's withdrawal in what one imagines to be both a physical and psychological sense makes Kate realise the 'worthlessness of the foam-effervescence' and that 'she did not really want it'. What she receives instead is a 'new, soft, heavy, hot flow, when she was like a fountain gushing noiseless'. In words which are all too suggestive of the much-disputed distinction Freud makes between clitoral and vaginal orgasm, we are told that this was 'so different from the beak-like friction of Aphrodite of the foam, the friction which flares out in circles of phosphorescent ecstasy, to the last wild spasm which utters the involuntary cry, like a death-cry, the final love-cry'. She may have had this with Joachim but with Cipriano it was all so 'curiously beyond her knowing: so deep and hot and flowing, as it were subterranean'.[21]

There is here none of the mutual delectation in one another's bodies which Will and Anna Brangwen enjoy at a certain period in their marriage, but then neither is there much sign of that 'abiding place' which Ramón was looking for in his relations with Carlota. It seems rather as if Cipriano has decided that, if there is no real alternative between ravishing or being ravished, he was going to do the ravishing. Back in Italy, Lawrence had once confided to Compton Mackenzie how anxious it made him that he and Frieda almost never reached their climax at the same time.[22] It seems here as if he is indulging in a male fantasy which removes that problem for good. But Kate is not entirely convinced and it is agreed that she will go back to Europe to see her children before committing herself finally to Cipriano. There are nevertheless strong indications that she is ready to return shortly and become to Cipriano very much what Ramón has found in Theresa, the new young wife he has taken after Carlota has died and who is every unreconstructed male's dream of the perfectly submissive, supportive and yet not entirely colourless female partner. In the new world Ramón and Cipriano are seeking to establish, the man is indeed lord and master, not only in all political matters but crucially in the bedroom also where a deeper, more rich satisfaction is promised to the woman if she will only accept that sex is a matter for the man to control and not try to run things herself.

MILLETT AND MISOGYNY

There are memorable evocations of Mexican daily life in *The Plumed Serpent,* and enough fine descriptions of the local scenery and wild life to make E. M. Forster's claim that it was the finest of Lawrence's novels just about understandable.[23] Yet the political system Ramón and Cipriano are attempting to install has been rightly characterised as utopian, and the way women feature in it is likely to strike most readers nowadays as very unpleasant. In the early 1960s, when Lawrence was sometimes put forward as a prominent champion of sexual liberation, the incongruity of his appearance in this role made him vulnerable to attack. One of the first to recognise this was Kate Millett who, in a chapter of *Sexual Politics* in 1970, delivered several heavy blows from which his reputation has still not recovered.

One curiosity of Millett's chapter is that she concentrates her heaviest fire on a novella Lawrence wrote, not (as she claims) as a sequel to *The Plumed Serpent* but after he had finished *Quetzalcoatl*, and while he was back in New Mexico. This is called *The Woman Who Rode Away* and, thanks to Millett, it has received more attention, or notoriety, than it perhaps deserves. The stimulus of the novella was a visit with the woman who was now Mabel Luhan to a ceremonial cave of the Indians quite close to Taos. When Lawrence saw it there was a stream of water pouring down in front of the cave but Mabel pointed out that, in winter, this stream turned into a stalactite of ice and there was a moment of the day when the sun would shine through it to illuminate what might have been the cave's altar. It is here that Lawrence imagines the largely anonymous 'woman' of his title about to be sacrificed by a tribe of Indians she has herself deliberately sought out. They have mistaken her for the mysterious stranger who figures in their mythology as someone willing to sacrifice herself to their gods, and thereby allow them to recover the powers of the sun and moon wrested from them by the white races. Interested as he was in Aztec religion, Lawrence must have felt an obligation to try to see from the inside, as it were, the most repellent and apparently unimaginable of its religious practices. Of course, Millett is right to assume that the gender of the victim – whose half acquiescence in her fate is shown to be *not only* the result of the drugs she is given – is no accident; and she highlights the moment when, as the sacrifice is about to take place,

Lawrence observes: 'The sharpness and the quivering nervous consciousness of the highly bred white woman was to be destroyed again, womanhood was to be cast once more into the great stream of impersonal sex and impersonal passion'.[24] Yet this hardly seems to justify her accusing Lawrence of 'pandering to a pornographic dream', or writing a novella which is 'sadistic pornography' when sex plays only a minor role in it. A prominent feature is in fact the total lack of interest the Indians display in the woman as a sexual being, even when they strip her of her Western clothes in order to dress her in ceremonial garments. According to Millett, however, the 'barbaric ecstasy' of those who officiate at the sacrifice is sexual as 'they await the moment when the sun, phallic itself, strikes the phallic icicle, and signals the phallic priest to plunge the phallic knife – penetrating the female victim and cutting out her heart – the death fuck'.[25] Critical of Freud as Millett is elsewhere in her book, she is more than a little reliant on a vulgarisation of Freud's notions of sexual symbolism here. For her, 'The Woman Who Rode Away' can be associated with a common fantasy of the Western world whereby the white woman is captured by savages and forced 'to live in a state of utter humiliation and abjection, raped, beaten, tortured, finally stripped and murdered'.[26] But in Lawrence's story the woman is treated with the certain amount of reverence which her status as a vitally important sacrificial victim requires, and she is neither raped, nor beaten, nor tortured (although she is of course murdered).

Millett has many true things to say in her chapter and deserves credit for trying to bring them to the attention of a public with a false idea of Lawrence, but she spoils their effect by overplaying her hand; or perhaps it is because she overplays her hand that her chapter has been so effective. Her critical method is hard to illustrate briefly but a short example of it can be found in the footnote she attaches to the sentences above about what happens to white women who are captured by savages:

Lawrence has a number of stories like this: *None of That* is a grim little piece of hate about an American woman who is gang-raped by a group of shoddy toreadors in gratitude for the fortune she wills to one of them; *The Princess* gives an account of a Mexican guide who rapes and imprisons an American in the mountains – a story done with infinite malice and sexual enmity. There is a premonition of the Lawrence who wrote *The Woman Who Rode Away* as early as *Sons and Lovers*, when little Paul Morel suggests 'Let's make a sacrifice of Arabella … Let's burn her'. Having found her face 'stupid' he stands by, watching with satisfaction while the figure melts, then takes the charred remains and smashes them with stones. Annie whose only toy this had been, stands by helpless and understandably disturbed while Paul shouts, 'That's the sacrifice of Misses Arabella … And I'm glad there's nothing left of her.' [27]

None of That! is a short but complicated story written well after Lawrence had left North America although the central female figure is given the physical appearance, and many of the psychological characteristics, of Mabel Luhan. She is a woman of enormous willpower who is looking for a man to match her own energy and drive. Living in Mexico, she goes to watch a famous bull fighter and is as fascinated by the dominance and skill he demonstrates as Gudrun is by Gerald's control of his horse. She becomes obsessed with him even though, or perhaps because, he is a boorish, entirely instinctive individual without imagination. After repeated meetings in the safety of where she herself is staying, during which she fails to recruit him to her own scale of values, she agrees to a late-night rendezvous in his own house where he does indeed hand her over to a group of his bull-fighting entourage. There are no details of the rape – the whole story is in reported speech and was claimed by Lawrence to have been based on fact [28]– but it nonetheless constitutes a shocking conclusion to the story and makes it as 'grim' as

Millett claims it to be. After the rape the woman commits suicide but leaves a note in which she insists that the generous provision she had *already made* for the bullfighter in her will should stand.[29] The crudely misleading summary of *None of That!* which Millett offers here is therefore the least inaccurate part of her footnote, with the prize for what is the most going to the references to *Sons and Lovers*. What she forgets to say in those is that young Paul is consumed with guilt because he is the one who has broken his sister's doll. Destroying it as completely as he then does is a confused child's way of finding an object which allows him to revenge himself for the acute discomfort he is experiencing. However much some would like to apply this model to the way Lawrence himself dealt with the guilt involved in abandoning Jessie Chambers,[30] Paul's actions have at this stage in his life nothing to do with misogyny. That the doll of his sister should be female is after all hardly surprising.[31]

The Princess has a setting in New Mexico and, like *The Woman Who Rode Away*, was written there. It concerns a woman of diminutive physique whose father is the head of a Scottish clan and who provides her with all the material and emotional support she needs. When he dies she thinks vaguely of replacing him with a husband and, finding herself in the States (her mother's country), becomes interested in a Mexican who is acting as a guide on a 'dude ranch' in New Mexico, and who was formerly the owner of the land he now shows to visitors (so that if she is a princess, as her father liked to call her, he is a dispossessed prince). The woman deliberately contrives to go alone with this man on a long and partly symbolic trip into territory whose wildness both intrigues and frightens her. The two of them spend the night in a hut and, when she is woken by the cold, she agrees that she would like him to 'make [her] warm'.[32] What follows satisfies her curiosity but only by convincing her how alien sexual activity is to her nature. The bluntness with which she makes that clear to the Mexican the next morning so wounds his masculine pride that he throws her clothes in a lake and forces her to have sex with him again on the assumption he can somehow make her appreciative. When two Rangers appear on the scene he shoots at them and is then shot himself. The power and effectiveness of this story derives from an even distribution of sympathy. The reader is made to understand Romero's fierce resentment, which is political as well as sexual, without in any way finding it attractive; but is also led to recognise that his death is a direct consequence of the woman's failure properly to understand her own sexual nature. To say, therefore, that the story is written 'with infinite malice and sexual enmity' is a misrepresentation almost as grotesque as drawing a parallel between Paul's sacrifice of Arabella and the fate of the woman who rode away. There is certainly a strong misogynist thread running through much of what Lawrence wrote in Mexico and America, but characterising it is a more complicated business than Millett imagined.

THE PRE-SEXUAL WORLD

The Princess and *The Woman Who Rode Away* belong to a trio of novellas with New Mexican settings, the third of which is *St. Mawr*. But this last story is also the result of Lawrence's visit back to Europe in the winter of 1923–4. He had been planning to return there in August 1923, in part because Frieda was so anxious to see her second child, Elsa, whose approaching twenty-first birthday meant that the legal barriers which her father had erected to prevent any contacts between her and her mother were no longer operative. But Lawrence had always been disturbed by his wife's continuing attachment to her children and decided to exert that mastership which he felt a husband ought to enjoy in marriage by changing his mind at the last minute. The result was that Frieda decided she would make the trip alone, and that the Lawrences began what was not merely a period away from each other, but something more like a formal separation. There was a contest of wills which, after trailing rather miserably across the United States to California, and then down back to Mexico, Lawrence had to admit he had lost when in November he took a boat from Veracruz and went to rejoin his wife.

Set in Shropshire, the first and best part of *St. Mawr* is a savage satire on the upper echelons of English village society. The criticism is channelled through a formidable middle-aged American woman, Mrs. Witt, who is, in her energy and will, rather like the protagonist in *None of That!*. Not exempt from satire herself – as an American aristocrat from New Orleans, she expects young men to be 'as democratic as Abraham Lincoln and as aristocratic as a Russian Czar' – she functions as a withering *spectator ab extra*, thinking of Texas as she sarcastically endorses the local Dean's characterisation of his village as 'isolated' ten miles from Shrewsbury, and commenting, when she decides to provide the local pub with a weekly barrel of beer which the landlord can sell to his working-class clientele at only a penny a glass, 'My own country has gone dry, but not because we can't *afford* it'. The daughter of Mrs. Witt is called Lou and married to Rico, a handsome socialite whose inadequacies are exposed when he fails to control a stallion the couple have bought for riding in Hyde Park (it is the name of this horse which provides the novella with its title). Horses are often symbols of sexual potency in Lawrence and this one does so much damage that plans are made to have him gelded. Mother and daughter therefore remove St. Mawr to the States where they finally settle on a ranch in New Mexico, the detailed description of which makes it identical to the one which had been given to Frieda by Mabel Luhan. There Lou declares that 'either my taking a man shall have a meaning and a mystery that penetrates my very soul, or I will keep to myself'. When her mother replies, in her usual sardonic manner, that she might therefore find that she has to keep to herself for good, Lou says,

Do you think I mind! There's something else for me, mother. There's something else even that loves and wants me. I can't tell you what it is. It's a spirit. And it's here, on this

ranch. It's here, in this landscape. It's something more real
to me than men are, and it soothes me, and it holds me up
…It needs me. It craves for me. And to it, my sex is deep
and sacred, deeper than I am, with a deep nature aware
deep down of my sex.[33]

This is the erotic relationship with Nature which Somers has entered into towards the end of *Kangaroo*, but here Lawrence imagines
it from a female point of view.

Throughout his career Lawrence wrote essays as well as fiction. In 1925 he published a collection of these under the title
Reflections on the Death of a Porcupine. Some of the items he included were quite old, like the essay on 'Love' which had first
appeared in the *English Review* in 1918. He was struggling there
with his usual problem of how, in a relationship with a woman, a
man can both surrender himself and retain his own being. In the
fire of 'extreme sensual love' he writes:

> in the friction of intense, destructive flames, I am destroyed
> and reduced to essentiality: she is destroyed and reduced
> to her essential otherness. It is a destructive fire, this pro-
> fane love. But it is the only fire that will purify us into
> singleness, fuse us from the chaos into our own gem-like
> separateness of being.[34]

Seven years afterwards, in an essay written while he was in New
Mexico and called '….Love Was Once a Little Boy', which is also
included in the *Reflections* volume, it is clear Lawrence no longer
believes that sexual intercourse is the royal road to an intensified
individuality:

> Most of our talk about love is cant, and bunk. The trea-
> sure of treasures to man and woman today is his, or her
> own ego. And this ego, each hopes it will flourish like a

salamander in the flame of love and passion. Which it well may: but for the fact that there are two salamanders in the same flame, and they fight till the flame goes out. Then they become grey cold lizards of the vulgar ego.[35]

Having dealt with human relationships in his first two pages of his new essay, and to some extent therefore with his relationship to Frieda, Lawrence turns with evident relief to discuss a cow called Susan which he had acquired for the ranch. The beauty of his descriptions of Susan indicates how important it is for him to establish a satisfactory relationship with her, as with all the other manifestations of Nature which surround him in New Mexico. He feels he has contrived to do this, if only intermittently, meeting Susan in that third realm which, in an essay called 'Morality and the Novel' (not in this collection), he had described as also the home of the genuine work of art, the work of art, that is, which is neither Van Gogh's perception of the sunflowers nor the sunflowers themselves, but 'a revelation of a perfect relation, at a certain moment, between a man and a sunflower'.[36]

Recognition of his success with Susan leads Lawrence to a criticism of Wordsworth in his relation to Nature. He remembers from school (as either pupil or teacher) the famous lines about Peter Bell for whom 'A primrose by the river's brim / A yellow primrose was to him / And nothing more' and assumes it was Wordsworth's intention to contrast Peter's indifference to the natural world with the solipsistic quality of his own attention: 'The yokel had no relation at all – or next to none – with the primrose. William gathered it to his bosom and made it part of his own nature'. Warming to his theme, and after having made his own contribution to the long list of parodies of *Peter Bell*, he complains, 'Ah, William! The "something more" that the primrose was to you, was yourself in the mirror'.[37] Towards the end of '….Love Was Once a Little Boy', he returns to the issue once more and lights on a striking if misapplied phrase: 'So a man can go forth in desire, even to a primrose. But let him refrain from falling over the poor blossom, as William did. Or trying to incorporate into his own ego, which is a sort of lust. Nasty anthropomorphic lust'.[38] Memorable though this last phrase is, the charge is unjust since Wordsworth was as aware as Lawrence of his own solipsistic tendencies and works hard, in *The Prelude* especially, to reach that stage where his mind is 'creator and receiver both, / Working but in alliance with the works / Which it beholds'. If there is anthropomorphic lust, therefore, it is less in *his* poetry than in Lou's belief in *St. Mawr* that the landscape around has a craving for her, and a deep awareness of her sex. What seems rather to be involved in her case is what I have called the auto-eroticism of Birkin rolling in the wet grass or (as I said) Somers by the sea-shore.

Not all the landscape described at the end of *St. Mawr* is associated with sex. Figuring quite prominently, for example, is a pine tree near the ranch which is clearly the same as the one Lawrence describes several times in his letters or non-fictional writing. In the novella, it becomes a 'passionless non-phallic column, rising in the shadows of the pre-sexual world, before the hot-blooded ithyphallic column ever erected itself'.[39] These are difficult words – what world could it be in which there is no reproduction and how could it continue? – but echoes of them can be found in a short story Lawrence began writing in 1924 while he was still in Europe and probably completed once he was back in New Mexico. It chiefly concerned Middleton Murry, who had been his closest friend in the years before the outbreak of the war, and for several more thereafter. They quarrelled often and an apparently definitive break came after Lawrence had sent a cruelly abusive note to Murry's wife, Katherine Mansfield, as she was dying of consumption. When Frieda returned to Europe in 1923 she had, however, re-established contact with Murry, whose wife was now dead, in a manner which excited Lawrence's jealousy and suspicion over what had transpired before he chose to rejoin her. 'The Border-Line' is a story about a woman with many of Frieda's characteristics who has lost her husband in the war and is travelling through Europe to a romantic rendezvous with one of his former friends. When, however, she is about to make love to this man the ghost of her husband, which has been hovering in the vicinity, pushes the other man out of bed so that he can perform that function himself. It is then she discovers that 'he was hard and cold like a tree, and alive. And the prickling of his moustache was the cold prickling of fir-needles. He held her fast and hard, and seemed to possess her through every pore of her body. Not now the old, procreative way of possession'.[40] Puzzling as this is, it would seem to elucidate, or at least help to elucidate, the reference to the pre-sexual world in the description of the pine tree in *St. Mawr*, and Lawrence becomes more specific as he elaborates on the former husband's way of making love:

> And again, as he pressed her fast, and pressed his cold face against her, it was as if the wood of the tree itself were growing round her, the hard live wood compressing and almost devouring her, the sharp needles brushing her face, the limbs of the living tree enveloping her in the last, final ecstasy of submission, squeezing from her the last drop of her passion, like the cold white berries of mistletoe on the tree of life.[41]

Lawrence had several advantages over Murry which are highlighted in how the friend of the heroine's former husband is described in 'The Border-Line'. He was, for example, taller and he did not have a bald spot. Yet in one crucial respect he may well have been conscious of himself as inferior. Whether the tuberculosis which was to be officially diagnosed in Mexico City in March 1925 had made him impotent, or he had simply lost interest, it is reasonably certain that for some time he had not had regular sexual relations with Frieda whereas Murry was certainly both capable of and ready for them. The alternative to penetrative sex which Lawrence offers in 'The Border-Line', and declares superior, is very

strange indeed. His fiction of this period features a good number of middle-aged women who are still full of energy and refuse to retire from the sexual field gracefully. Although a model for these characters can often be found in Mabel Luhan and her female friends, it is evident that Frieda also sometimes made a contribution. Here, however, the husband whom the female protagonist thought was dead squeezes the last drop of passion out of her so that she is in an 'ecstasy of final submission'. The powers he is able to call upon to achieve this result are implicitly characterised by Lawrence as belonging to a pre-sexual world, but the terms in which it is described are sexual enough to suggest fantasies of compensation. Cipriano has phallic powers which reduce the opposite sex to 'prone submission' but the dead husband of the protagonist of 'The Border-Line' brings from another world non-phallic forces which Lawrence imagines as equally, if not more effective.

CHAPTER FIVE:
A CHANGE OF HEART

THE VIRGIN AND THE GIPSY

When Lawrence went back to Europe for good in 1925, it meant a return to Frieda's children. He had always steadily opposed the idea that a family was what sex, and by extension marriage, was really for. That Frieda could never quite recover from having been forced to leave her three offspring behind when she parted from her husband enraged him. She had made a crucial life decision to commit herself to him, he felt, and ought to be prepared to accept the consequences without repining. Explaining his refusal to accompany her on her trip back from New York in 1923 he wrote to Murry, 'F. wants to see her children. And you know, wrong or not, I can't stomach the chasing of those Weekley children'.[1] Yet once he was back in Europe permanently, and his wife's son and daughters had turned into young adults, he gradually found he got on with them quite well. This was particularly the case with the youngest, Barbara, or Barby as she was always known. The most rebellious of the three, and the one whom her father felt was most likely to have inherited Frieda's 'bad blood' (she had been expelled from her English public school for drawing male nudes in a textbook), Barby became an art student and saw a lot of her mother and second husband. It was through her that Lawrence was able to increase his knowledge of the post-war 'flapper' generation, with its cropped hair for women, fashions in which far more flesh was exposed than had ever been the case in the recent past, apparently wild, orgiastic dances, and a much more relaxed attitude to the mingling of the sexes. The consequence was a number of short stories and articles by Lawrence in his last years in which he expressed limited approval of a relaxation in the standards that had been set by people like his mother in the years before the war but, at the same time, scepticism about the authenticity of the new openness, and an anxious conservatism as to where it would all lead.

A late example of his interest in the new generation is an article he wrote, but never managed to publish, called 'Making Love to Music'. In this he begins by observing that the words of his title had been put forward as an apt definition of dancing, and goes on to contrast the 'smart and bouncing' country dances of his great-grandmother's generation, which 'worked up the blood and danced a man nearer and nearer to copulation', with the modern variety surprisingly and inexplicably characterised by him as 'distinctly anti-sexual'. 'We would say,' he writes, that 'modern jazz and tango and Charleston, far from being an incitement to copulation, are in direct antagonism to copulation' (both the two-step and the black bottom also receive a mention from him in this context). Lawrence offers only the shadow of an argument in justification of his distinction which seems to have been introduced chiefly so that he can sing the praises of the dancers he had seen depicted in the Etruscan tombs he had only recently visited:

> There the painted women dance, in their transparent linen with heavier, coloured borders, opposite the naked-limbed men, in a splendour and an abandon which is not at all abandoned. ... They are wild with a dance that is heavy and light at the same time, and not a bit anti-copulative, yet not bouncingly copulative either.[2]

The good thing about the Etruscans, he felt, was that there were phallic and womb symbols everywhere in their culture, so much a part of everyday life that there was no need to get sex 'on the brain, as we tend to do'. This meant they could dance with genuine freedom and not find themselves being bounced towards copulation, like the great-grandmothers, or 'sliding and shaking and waggling to elude it', like the members of Barby's generation.[3]

The decorated Etruscan tombs were a revelation to Lawrence. They seemed to suggest a people who so much enjoyed themselves that, rather than becoming solemn and miserable at the thought of death, were willing to extend that enjoyment into their conception of the after-life. A representative figure for him, as it has been for so many visitors to Tarquinia since, was the naked man in the so-called hunting and fishing frieze who is taking a perpendicular plunge into the sea with a huge grin on his face. A distinctive feature of Etruscan culture, in contrast to that of the Romans who conquered them, appears to have been that women mingled freely with men in their festivities. In describing a representation of one of these, Lawrence lights on a value which would become very important to him in his final years:

> On the end wall is a gentle little banqueting scene, the bearded man softly touching the woman with him under the chin, a slave boy standing childishly behind, and an alert dog under the couch … Rather gentle and lovely is the way he touches the woman under the chin, with a delicate caress. That again is one of the charms of the etruscan paintings, they really have the sense of touch …It is one of the rarest qualities, in life as in art. There is plenty of pawing and laying hold, but no real touch … Here, in this faded etruscan painting, there is the quiet flow of touch that unites the man and woman on the couch, the timid boy behind, the dog that lifts his nose, even the very garlands that hang from the wall.[4]

In 1919, Lawrence had written a short story in which a woman who is declining into spinsterhood strokes by mistake the face of a young man while he is asleep with the result that, once properly awake, he insists she must marry him.[5] It was his own morbid distaste for being touched in the wrong way, pawed and laid hold of, to use the language employed here, which made the medical inspections he was obliged to endure during the war such a night-mare for him. But in the Etruscans he felt he had found a people who, largely because they were so at ease with sex, knew how to touch each other in the right way. This was a complete change of paradigm after the fierce Aztecs, and although he had certainly been fascinated by the various Indian dances he had seen in the Taos pueblo and elsewhere in New Mexico, and in articles such as 'The Hopi Snake Dance' had written very well about them,[6] what he imagined as Etruscan dancing had a liveliness and life-enhanc-ing quality that had a special appeal for him.

Lawrence's thoughts on dancing post-date *Lady Chatterley's Lover*. Since this novel marks such a crucial change in his attitudes, anything Barby Weekley had to tell or show him about the new generation becomes less important than the significant if indirect role she played in its composition. As early as the time she spent with him and Frieda in Italy at the end of 1925 and beginning of 1926, she must have talked about the way she had been looked af-ter by Weekley's relatives when she was growing up. These included an unmarried sister whom she particularly disliked and above all her father's mother, who seems to have been a fearsome matriarch. In *The Virgin and the Gipsy* Lawrence transposed these figures into a country vicarage and fashioned out of his own memories, Frieda's gossip and what Barby had to say a Church of England clergyman who recalls in many ways Ernest Weekley himself, especially in that he is described as having been used to calling his wife a 'snowflow-er', and had been deserted by her. 'When the vicar's wife went off with a young and penniless man', this novella begins, 'the scandal knew no bounds'.[7]

Lawrence's portraits of Anglican vicars are never very sympa-thetic, as *Daughters of the Vicar* illustrates. Like the Rev. Mr Lindley, the vicar in *The Virgin and the Gipsy* also has two daughters. In an indication of how this story modulates between realism and al-legory, he is called Saywell, and hides beneath a tolerant surface of conventional good manners a mean and timid spirit. But his

younger daughter, Yvette, suffers more from his blind old mother and especially his unmarried sister, Aunt Cissie. In Lawrence's
jaundiced view, spinsterhood was almost always synonymous with
repression of the sex instinct and must therefore result in either
illness or character distortion (a mean old maid is how he unfairly
and ignorantly characterised Jane Austen).[8] In scenes written with
powerful comic gusto, Aunt Cissie is shown suffering from a mysterious internal complaint and driven into impotent and envious
rage by Yvette's youth and her heedless behaviour. The girl herself
finds the young men of her own class with whom she associates
unsatisfactory, but she is intrigued by a gipsy, temporarily in the
neighbourhood, and, even though he is married, it is in his cara-
van that she comes very close to having her first sexual experience.
Later she is back in the rectory when the heavy rains of previous
weeks precipitate a flood that threatens to sweep the whole building away. Her life is saved by the fortuitous arrival of the gipsy who
helps her to struggle upstairs to a room protected from the force of
the rushing water by its closeness to the chimney breast; and who
then, having taken off his own sodden clothes, holds her naked
body against his in order to protect her from hypothermia and the
effects of shock. Like the flood in one of Lawrence's favourite books
from his youth, *The Mill on the Floss*, this episode is both realistic
and allegorical. Before the water arrives there are several references
to the Lady of Shallot with Yvette described as looking out of the
rectory in the vague hope of seeing the gipsy's cart pass by, and by
having the flood sweep through the rectory, taking with it the old
grandmother, Lawrence suggests an end to its airless and stuffy con-
formity. The gipsy initiates Yvette into a new life, bringing to her
a human warmth which has been notably lacking in the potently
evoked domestic staleness of her environment; but he does so in a
way which is sufficiently symbolic – whether or not he and the girl
actually have sex is never clear – that readers are discouraged from
wondering whether such a relationship with an educated, middle-
class girl could be sustained. It is only in the aftermath of the flood,

and when he has left the neighbourhood, that Yvette even becomes aware that he has a name.[9]

THE FIRST LADY CHATTERLEY

The Virgin and the Gipsy exhibits important although still small signs of a substantial change in Lawrence's attitude to sexual relations, if that is what Yvette and the gipsy do indeed have. While he was in North America he appears to have wanted to write about the subjection of women, and how sexual intercourse can bring them to accept male dominance. This was associated with a political programme which insisted on the folly of assuming that all men were equal, and the need any society has for hierarchy and leadership. After *The Plumed Serpent* had been published, and perhaps as a minor consequence of living in Mussolini's Italy, he grew away from these beliefs, and when an American friend questioned the novel's politics admitted that, on the whole, he agreed that 'the leader-cum-follower relationship is a bore. And the new relationship will be some sort of tenderness, sensitive, between men and men and men and women, and not the one up one down, lead on I follow, ich dien sort of business'.[10] His remarks illustrate the beginnings of the change of heart which becomes more evident in the attempt he made shortly after completing *The Virgin and the Gipsy* to rewrite that story in a more realistic mode. This is the not quite complete typescript known as *The First Lady Chatterley* and at one moment in it the eponymous heroine (who now no longer bears any relation to Barby) has become pregnant. Although the pregnancy has occurred with her crippled and impotent husband's modified approval, it is felt at first that it would be best to hide from him that the father is his own gamekeeper, who is known in this preliminary version of the novel as Parkin. Duncan Forbes, a middle-class friend who has toyed with the idea of falsely assuming that responsibility, meets up with Parkin and, in the course of their conversation, says, 'I've hated democracy since the war. But now I see I'm wrong calling for an aristocracy. What we want is a flow of life from one to another'.[11] This sounds very much like Lawrence, the same Lawrence who would later be so excited by the Etruscan wall paintings. It is significant that one of his projected titles for *The First Lady Chatterley* was *Tenderness*.

Although *The First Lady Chatterley* takes up several of the themes of *The Virgin and the Gipsy*, its heroine is not of course a virgin, technically speaking; she has only become 'virgin by disuse' (to employ Lawrence's own phrase)[12] because her husband, Clifford Chatterley, has returned from the war paralysed from the waist down. Her sexual frustration leads her to have violent dreams of horses and she gets up in the morning with – according to what was in Lawrence's view almost always the result of repression – 'a terrible anger upon her, so that if she had not controlled herself, she could have bullied the servants cruelly, and have spoken to Clifford in savage derision'. Connie is in urgent need of what the gamekeeper can supply but he is an uneducated individual, with little or no interest in the arts or conversation. Although he is described as a kind of 'black man of the woods' for the local children and living in a cottage which has 'a certain fairy-tale atmosphere' about it,[13] this first version of *Lady Chatterley* is realist in the sense that in it Lawrence faces up to the issue of compatibility (as he had once done in the first version of *Daughters of the Vicar*). This is a problem that does not arise in the novella where a single contact is enough to save Yvette from her environment, just as one kiss from the Prince awakens the Sleeping Beauty. After Parkin has been forced to give up being a gamekeeper because of the scandals caused in Tevershall by Bertha Coutts, the wife from whom he has separated, he takes a job in a Sheffield steel works and lodges with a working-class family there called the Tewsons. Connie's visit to take tea with them and Parkin exposes any illusion she or the reader may still harbour that love (and sex) can easily conquer all, and that social differences do not matter. The scene is exceptionally well written, so much so that it becomes hard for Lawrence to find a convincing conclusion for his novel, which may be one of the reasons why he began to rewrite it almost immediately.

So incompatible do Connie and Parkin often seem to her that she is inclined to feel that she needs both him and Clifford in her life: 'Her two men were two halves. And she did not want to forfeit either half, to forego either man'.[14] These are very unusual sentiments for Lawrence to give to an essentially positive character. In the chapter in *Kangaroo* entitled 'Harriett and Lovatt at Sea in Marriage' he had concluded that, after the evaporation of 'perfect love', there was a choice between the wife accepting her husband's lord and mastership and her becoming his true friend and companion. This latter role would presumably include shared interests, mutual support and common memories, as the fervour of the first contacts modulated into something like affection or fondness. It was this idea of a married couple to which Lawrence seems to have been instinctively opposed; and he was sarcastic about members of Barby's generation who declared they were good friends with the boys they dated, perhaps because their attitude represented a diminution in the mystery and challenge of the opposite sex. But here Connie is contemplating a situation where Clifford offers all the qualities of companionship while Parkin supplies what her husband no longer can. For after all, if she and Parkin actually lived together 'they would humiliate one another. She, because she was in another world of culture than his – and he, because his state of nature would ignore so much of her.'[15]

Connie's belief that she needs both Clifford and Parkin in her life does not last much beyond the first half of *The First Lady Chatterley*, and for obvious reasons. In the first place it is identical to what becomes, as the novel evolves, one of Clifford's own preferred solutions to the dilemma in which he finds himself. If Connie is the kind of woman who cannot do without sex, then he is increasingly shown as willing to countenance the idea that she should take a lover. But this is in the context of a scenario where sex is little more than an appetite like hunger, which needs satisfying for reasons of the body's health, the kind of adjunct it was for Stendhal, for example, when he wrote his book on love. That work was a consequence of his unrequited passion for a woman called Métilde Dembouski and his standing in her eyes was not improved when a malicious friend revealed that, after leaving her Milanese *salon* late at night, he would sometime go off to seek the company of women who were more accommodating. That on the very same day he conceived the idea of writing *De l'amour* as a way of appealing indirectly to Métilde, he also discovered that he had contracted a venereal disease from one of these women did not trouble him unduly.[16] This was because love was separated in his mind from sex as a biological need, as it was for many others in his generation. By convincing herself that she needs both Clifford and Parkin, Connie is implicitly endorsing such a view, and at the same time demeaning the latter. At one moment in *The First Lady Chatterley*, Parkin asks what he would be called in her kind of language: "'My lover!", she stammered. "Lover!", he re-echoed. A queer flash went over his face. "Fucker!", he said, and his eyes darted a flash at her, as if he shot her'.[17] In his resentment, Parkin makes a particularly clear distinction between love and sex, and exposes the essentially unLawrentian way in which her idea for living with both men relegates sex to a function.

What quickly makes the idea of sharing her life between Clifford and Parkin impossible for Connie is the transformative nature of sexual intercourse with the gamekeeper. After her first orgasm, she feels 'filled … with unspeakable pleasure, a pleasure which has no contact with speech. She felt herself filled with new blood, as if the blood of the man had swept into her veins like a strong, fresh, rousing wind, changing her whole self. All her self felt alive, and in motion, like the woods in spring.' A little later, she describes herself as 'like the woman who touched Jesus. You touch the living body, and the flow starts in you, the dead flux dries up'.[18] The religious reference is not inappropriate given George Neville's suggestion, in his memoir, that Lawrence was always likely to approach sex as

if it were a sacrament.[19] Just over half way through *The First Lady Chatterley* there is a passage in which Connie decides that 'with the mystery of the phallos goes all the beauty of the world' and that it is 'the penis which connects us sensually with the planets'.[20] This gives to sex a meaning which is religious in the broadest sense of that term, and similar to the one Lawrence implies the Etruscans entertained when they worshipped the phallus as one of the two sources of all that exists (no talk now of a world that is *pre*-sexual). But these are ideas which cannot be reconciled with functional sex, the kind that does no more than conveniently offer release, and it is after having entertained them that Connie determines not to hand over the child she is going to have by Parkin to Clifford: 'It shall *not* be a Chatterley and baronet and a gentleman and another cold horror'. When Clifford suggests to her that since Mohammed, unlike Jesus, had several wives, he could have had no objection to sex, she implies that if the woman whom Jesus told to go and sin no more had said to him, 'Come thou, and sin with me!' it would have been better for all concerned.[21]

Lawrence had objections to the puritanical, Pauline elements in Christianity which only strengthened as he grew older; and he found it regrettable for Western culture as a whole that its founder is depicted as having had no sexual experience. Shortly after his Etruscan tour, he wrote the first half of a novella called *The Escaped Cock* in which the story of the Resurrection is movingly told with details that only someone who was himself periodically experiencing painful minor recoveries from a debilitating, incurable illness could supply. The title of this work was inspired by a model of a white rooster escaping from an egg which he had seen in Volterra and had at this stage little to do with sex. That changed when Lawrence later supplied the story with a second half in which the central figure from the first takes shelter in a temple presided over by a young Priestess of Isis, the Egyptian goddess who is in search of the scattered parts of the body of her brother, Osiris, so that she can reassemble them and bring fertility to the land. The Indians in *The Woman Who Rode Away* mistake their American intruder for the white visitor who will restore the fortunes of their race. With much happier results, the Isis priestess assumes that the resurrected Christ figure, with his scars and scarcely healed wounds, is the lost Osiris. Her tender desire has a healing effect and touches even the man who is so recently risen from the dead that he has wanted to avoid any close human contact (*'Noli me tangere'*). With oil, she massages the wound in the man's side and all his lower body so that (in the old phrase) his loins stir. The resurrection of the body of which the Bible speaks could or should, in Lawrence's view, always include the return of sexual desire and potency.[22]

For Connie, sex becomes so important that all the cultural and social advantages which Clifford might appear to offer cannot hold the balance for long. It is quite soon therefore that the idea she needs both men, involving as it does a new and unusual notion for Lawrence, disappears from *The First Lady Chatterley*; and there is certainly no more talk of companionship in its immediate sequel, the second version of the novel for which *John Thomas and Lady Jane* is only one of several titles he toyed with. But there is another idea which is also new in the first version that has a happier fate, and represents a potentially more lasting change in Lawrence's views. It is after all not only sex for which Connie is shown yearning, but also motherhood. That is not a feeling in women for which in the past Lawrence had shown a great deal of sympathy, but now he writes with sensitivity about a need which is not only for sex but its consequences. That element in *The First Lady Chatterley*, far from disappearing, becomes more prominent until it could be said to culminate in the moving scenes in the novel's final version where Connie goes into the wood to see the new-born chicks and experiences acutely 'the agony of her own female forlornness'.[23] Her feelings are then described with a 'tenderness' which would have justified the retention of that original title, for those parts of the completed novel at least.

EVOLUTION OF A NOVEL

One way in which the evolution of *Lady Chatterley's Lover* proceeds is by the rounding out of the characters. Mrs. Bolton, for example, the woman from the local community who is called in to look after Clifford, is only lightly sketched at first but becomes in the end a figure worthy of George Eliot. The setting for *Lady Chatterley's Lover* is heavily dependent on what proved to be Lawrence's last visit to his native regions in August and September of 1926; but that happened to coincide with a long miners' strike, an event which seems to have not only reinforced his own increasingly strong class antagonisms, but reminded him of what a class-ridden country England always was. Mrs. Bolton is deeply resentful of the bosses because they have misrepresented how her husband came to be killed in the pit more than twenty years before, making him seem like a coward. 'One part of me went with him', she explains to Connie, '…It was as if I could only feel his arms round me, an' his body against me, an' his legs against my legs. It's the touch of him that I can never really get over'. Connie's response is to ask whether that experience can be so durable: 'Can a man's touch on a woman last so long?', to which Mrs. Bolton replies that it can 'if it's the right man!'.[24] This exchange occurs in the novel's second version but it is similar in the final one and important in reaffirming that Lawrence does not conceive of satisfactory sexual relations between a man and a woman as a necessarily on-going process. To have them at one period of a life may be enough, as Paul Morel suggests it was for his mother, but what Lawrence is increasingly keen to stress is that, with Clifford, Connie never had them at all.

Perhaps the most important change which took place as Lawrence rewrote his novel was the elimination of that problem of compatibility with which he had begun by struggling. As Parkin evolves into Mellors, he turns out to have acquired both an education and a commission in the army. These have made him a perfect bi-lingual, able to converse with the middle and upper classes on their own terms but fall back into dialect whenever it suits him: that is, for either tender or (in the case of Connie's sister Hilda) distinctly untender purposes. What he and Connie would say to each other at meal-times if they lived together, which was one of the questions she had asked herself in *The First Lady Chatterley*, is therefore no longer a problem.

Changes are made to the presentation of Clifford of almost equal importance. In *A Propos of 'Lady Chatterley's Lover'* Lawrence was to point to a difficulty which had been with him from the beginning. 'I realised that it was perhaps taking an unfair advantage of Connie, to paralyse [Clifford] technically', he wrote. 'It made it so much more vulgar of her to leave him'.[25] He might have added that the difficulty was made more acute by Clifford's paralysis being a consequence of the war, and that many of his first readers would be aware of men in their immediate environment who had suffered in a similar way. The sympathy they might very naturally evoke is in conflict with the stern Nietzschean morality which tends to colour all Lawrence's treatments of disability, whether they are accidental, like Clifford's, or congenital like that of the unfortunate Mr. Massey, the curate with the body of a sickly lad of thirteen who marries the heroine's elder sister in *Daughters of the Vicar*. This insists that no injuries on the scale Clifford has suffered them are without corresponding psychological impairment, and that their victims therefore necessarily become a threat to the healthy and undamaged. There are glimpses of this attitude at the beginning of *The First Lady Chatterley* when Clifford is described as having features which are still sensitive and critical, but which also display something 'secretive and assertive, the peculiar assertion of the will-to-live, the right-to-exist, in the crippled man, that betrayed him, and gave him a hard, almost impudent expression'. Parkin can certainly be found in this version feeling that Clifford would be better off dead and a reason for this is stated more formally, in the final one, where we are told of Clifford that 'the paralysis, the bruise of the too-great shock was gradually spreading to his affective self'.[26]

That Lawrence himself shows scant sympathy for Clifford's injuries, and recognition of how they came about, does not make him oblivious to how differently certain of his readers might respond. But he has various ways of preventing them from taking too harsh a view of Connie's behaviour in deceiving and then leaving her husband, in addition to his illustration of the effect of sexual frustration on her own well-being and health. From the start, Clifford's bath chair has a motor attached to it and, as his interest in mining is developed, he becomes more and more the representative of industrialisation, eventually crushing the flowers in the wood as his machine rides over them in a memorable and effective scene in the final version. Yet as far as love and sex are concerned, the most prominent of Lawrence's methods for inhibiting sympathy is to suggest continually that Clifford had never been very interested in sex even before his injury, and for such a poor performer the paralysis of his genitalia is therefore no great loss. His increasing emergence as a mean-spirited snob does not help his cause either. In the final version he has become a fashionable, successful but fundamentally shallow writer and is surrounded by a group of friends, much developed from versions one and two, who radically change the dynamic of the novel. This is because they allow Lawrence to stage debates about sex which can act as a backdrop to Connie's discovery of its rewards and pleasures with the gamekeeper. Among this group he places a figure it is reasonable to regard as in many ways his own spokesman, a retired soldier called Tommy Dukes who characterises the freer attitude to love of the modern generation (Barby's contemporaries) as 'fellows with swaying waists fucking jazz girls with small boy buttocks' and champions the centrality of 'real sex'.[27] But others in the group treat sex in a much more casual way, as indeed does Clifford in a private conversation he has with Connie shortly after one of these debates:

> It is what endures through one's life, that matters ... what
> do the occasional connections matter? And the occasional

sexual connections especially! If people don't exaggerate
them ridiculously, they pass like the mating of birds. And
so they should. What does it matter! It's the life-long companionship that matters. It's the living together from day
to day, not the sleeping together once or twice … Little by
little, living together, two people fall into a sort of unison,
they vibrate so intricately to one another. That's the secret
of marriage, not sex; at least not the simple function of sex.
You and I are interwoven in a marriage. If we stick to that,
we ought to be able to arrange this sex thing, as we arrange
going to the dentist; since fate has given us a checkmate
physically there.[28]

Out of context, and forgetting the unfortunate remark about the
dentist, one might think Clifford talks reasonably here, given his
dilemma. But his is a position which everything in the final version
of the novel works to undermine; and its proponent is humiliated
when he is eventually shown fondling Mrs. Bolton's breasts as he
descends into infantilism, a scene written with such venom that it
could perhaps only have come from the pen of someone very much
aware of his own temptation to seek refuge from the world in the
comforts of an ample maternal bosom.[29]

In the 1950s Frieda made a startling observation about *Lady
Chatterley's Lover*. 'The terrible thing about Lady C', she wrote,
'is that L. identified himself with both Clifford and Mellors; that
took courage, that made me shiver, when I read it as he wrote
it'.[30] The implicit claim here is that in the last years of her marriage to Lawrence sexual relations between them had ceased and
he was impotent. This is certainly what she told one or two people
later, and she would have felt the second part of her claim was
confirmed had she known about what appears to have happened
between her husband and Dorothy Brett. This minor painter had
accompanied the Lawrences when they sailed back to the States
in March 1924 after their brief interlude in Europe. The idea was

that she would help to form a small community on the New Mexican ranch, once they had been joined by Middleton Murry (with whom she had recently had an affair). But Murry never fulfilled his promise to come and Brett (as she was always called) therefore attached herself to Lawrence and became his devoted admirer, very much to Frieda's annoyance. What she claimed to be irritated by was that the devotion never led anywhere, and the relationship of Brett and Lawrence was therefore like those platonic ones which she implied often develop between curates and their unmarried female parishioners. Once the Lawrences were back in Europe and living in Spotorno on the Italian Riviera, they had one of their periodic fierce quarrels and separations, with Lawrence going off to see some old friends in Capri. By this time Brett was also back in Europe and the two found themselves in adjoining rooms in the annex of a hotel in nearby Ravello.

The only account of what happened in Ravello came from Dorothy Brett almost fifty years later (after Frieda's death). According to her, on two successive nights Lawrence, having declared it was unnatural for intimate relationships between a man and woman not to have a physical consummation, came into her bedroom and tried but failed to make love to her, even though she felt 'an overwhelming desire to be adequate' and was 'passionately eager to be successful'. Some of the details she gives seem dubious but the general context in which she and Lawrence met, their relations in the past, and the letters he wrote to her after she had hurried away from Ravello immediately following the second night, strongly suggest the substance of what she says must be true.[31] Although this episode would not necessarily confirm Frieda's suggestion that her husband was impotent (not being able to make love to Brett does not inevitably mean he would have been incapable with someone else), she would have certainly taken it as doing so; and yet what she may also have been referring to when she claims he identified with Clifford was that her husband's departure from Spotorno left her freer to develop her relations with Angelo Ravagli, the landlord of the house in which the Lawrences had been living. Either then or shortly afterwards she began an affair with Ravagli which lasted the rest of her husband's life, and she took Angelo to New Mexico with her after Lawrence had died of tuberculosis in 1930. If Lawrence could identify with Clifford, therefore, it was (Frieda implies) because he also was not only impotent, but an impotent cuckold.

In *The First Lady Chatterley*, after Connie and Parkin have spent their first night together, she thinks of a well-known phrase from the Bible, 'And the grasshopper shall be a burden, and desire shall fail', pondering how awful it would be if desire did indeed fail.[32] Towards the very end of his life, Lawrence wrote a short poem in which he poignantly lamented, 'I cannot help but be alone / for desire has died in me, silence has grown, / and nothing now reaches out to draw / other flesh to my own'.[33] Yet whatever correspondence there was with Clifford in Lawrence seems to have intensified rather than lessened his hostility to the character (self-pity being one of the human weaknesses he most despised), and beside, as Frieda points out, he could also identify with Mellors. In that case, he was working from memory, recalling those early days with Frieda when, if the remark in *Mr. Noon* is to be believed, he could ejaculate three times in fifteen minutes. It may be there are fleeting allusions to how much things had changed since then when, in the first version of *Lady Chatterley*, he referred to how Clifford needed 'Constance's strange warm vagueness to keep his life warm. The women who didn't need sex and physical love just got on his nerves'; or, in the second, to 'rather elderly women, between forty and sixty' who were 'unscrupulous, and with a callousness that put the hyena to shame' and lusted to acquire 'a new grip over some man'. Towards the end of this second version, Connie asks Parkin not to betray what is between them. 'I don't even mind so *very* much if you go to other women, since you can't have me – if only you won't damage what is between you and me'.[34] This is the difficult distinction which Stendhal discusses in *De l'amour* between infidelity (casual affairs) and constancy. Well over a hundred years later, Lawrence may have been hoping that, although Frieda was unfaithful, she was nevertheless constant.

BEING EXPLICIT

The degree of expurgation which would have been necessary in order to have the first two versions of *Lady Chatterley* published in the usual way was not enormous. Both contain a scattering of what are known as the four-letter words but the descriptions of sexual intercourse in them are not too startlingly explicit. Lawrence had, however, spent all his publishing life expurgating and was sick of it. Settled in Florence for a while, he renewed his friendship with Norman Douglas who had published books there privately, and by subscription. It must have struck him that if he did the same, he could not only write whatever he liked but also perhaps make some money, an important consideration as his health continued to fail and he began wondering how Frieda was going to survive after his death (in fact, the privately published *Lady Chatterley's Lover* was eventually to make her a comparatively rich woman).

One of the important features of the sexual encounters of Connie and Mellors is that they usually take place either in the natural world or very close to it. A strong feeling for Nature and an ability to describe it were always one of Lawrence's greatest strengths. How much he excelled in that area becomes clear if he is compared with either of his two great rivals and contemporaries, Virginia Woolf and James Joyce. Only Proust displays a comparable sensitivity and knowledge. Situating Mellors and Connie so often in Nature creates the impression that their love-making is part of the natural cycle of things; like Paul Morel and Clara Dawes they include in their meetings 'the thrust of the manifold grass stems, the cry of the pewits, the wheel of the stars'. They are part of an annual cycle of renewal which Lawrence desperately hoped could also apply to him. The natural setting also helps to emphasise moments in the novel when Lawrence may be seeking to convey, not only what it

[handwritten margin note: in love is rare in Lawrence]

feels like to be sexually gratified, but also to be in love. As I said before, this aspect of human experience, which has been a major concern for very many writers in Western culture, is relatively rare in Lawrence. There is a point in *Women in Love* when Birkin remembers the beauty of Ursula's eyes, 'filled with light, like spring, suffused with wonderful promise' and tells her 'there is a golden light in you, which I wish you would give me'.[35] Brief, romantic moments of this kind are perhaps more frequent in *Lady Chatterley's Lover* than in any of Lawrence's previous novels and have combined with his vivid descriptions of the natural world, as the setting for the relationship of Connie and Mellors, to produce in some readers an impression of romantic pastoral. Yet it seem to me that, inspired though they may be by memories of the brief period when Lawrence could accurately be described as being in love with Frieda, these moments are far from frequent; and that it is only through wilful neglect of many other, more important aspects of the novel, that they can be made to constitute its predominant tone.

One certain task anyone who insisted on describing *Lady Chatterley's Lover* as a romantic pastoral novel would have to undertake is to remove from the first word any of the connotations it usually has with a certain dreamy vagueness. Being able to publish the novel privately meant that in his descriptions of sex Lawrence could be as precise and graphic as he liked and employ those words like cunt and fuck which, to echo again his defence of them in *A Propos of 'Lady Chatterley's Lover'*, are a 'natural part of the mind's consciousness of the body'. It is true that Connie's orgasms feature prominently in these descriptions, and they are of necessity highly metaphorical; and that there is in the novel a heavy concentration on feeling (especially hers). But when it comes to the more practical aspects of their love-making, he allows himself to be detailed and anatomical in a way which can surprise a reader even today. Features of Connie's naked body are often described but the best illustration is perhaps the vivid account of Mellors's erect and then detumescent penis, even though that raises difficulties quite apart from the issue of how truthful and realistic Lawrence was attempting to be, and is hard either to summarise or curtail:

> He slipped out of bed with his back to her, naked and white and thin, and went to the window, stooping a little, drawing the curtains and looking out for a moment. The back was white and fine, the small buttocks beautiful with an exquisite, delicate manliness, the back of the neck ruddy and delicate and yet strong. ...
>
> 'But you are beautiful', she said. 'So pure and fine! Come!' – She held her arms out.
>
> He was ashamed to turn on her, because of his aroused nakedness. He caught his shirt off the floor, and held it to him, coming to her.
>
> 'No!', she said, still holding out her beautiful slim arms from her drooping breasts. 'Let me see you!'
>
> He dropped his shirt and stood still, looking towards her. The sun through the low window sent in a beam that lit up his thighs and slim belly, and the erect phallus rising darkish and hot-looking from the little cloud of vivid gold-red hair. She was startled and afraid.
>
> 'How strange!' she said slowly. 'How strange he stands there! So big! and so dark and cock-sure! Is he like that?'
>
> The man looked down the front of his slender white body, and laughed. Between the slim breasts the hair was dark, almost black. But at the root of the belly, where the phallos rose thick and arching, it was gold-red, vivid in a little cloud.

There follows a short passage in which Mellors makes, in dialect, a partly comic address to his penis, instructing it to tell Connie that it is cunt he is after: 'Tell lady Jane tha wants cunt. John Thomas an' th' cunt o' lady Jane!'

'Oh, don't tease him,' said Connie, crawling on her knees on the bed towards him and putting her arms round his white slender loins, and drawing him to her so that her hanging swinging breasts touched the tip of the stirring, erect phallos, and caught the drop of moisture. She held the man fast.

'Lie down!', he said. 'Lie down! Let me come!'

He was in a hurry now.

And afterwards, when they were quite still, the woman had to uncover the man again, to look at the mystery of the phallos.

'And now he's tiny, and soft like a little bud of life!', she said, taking the soft small penis in her hand.[36]

In some ways this is an unrepresentative passage to choose in that sexual intercourse itself has been elided, and by the most traditional of means: that use of 'afterwards' on which Lawrence had so often had to rely in his previous novels. It is also not completely free of the circumlocutions which he had previously been obliged to employ, the example here being 'aroused nakedness'. And yet there is more than enough which is explicit to have made publication by the usual means quite impossible. Its directness makes the beam of light which shines through the window to light up Mellors's penis romantic in ways very different from what that word usually implies. When Kate Millett wrote her attack on Lawrence she began her chapter with this description and claimed, amongst several other charges, that it demonstrated its author's male narcissism. When there are signs of this in his early poetry the male narrator is referring to himself, whereas here the illuminated erect penis is viewed through the appreciative eyes of Connie. Although that may not be nearly enough to acquit the passage of a narcissistic tendency, it needs to be said that it is not characteristic of the novel as a whole and what distinguishes the eight accounts of Connie and Mellors having sex together is above all their variety. The only book as explicit as his own which Lawrence is likely to have read before writing *Lady Chatterley* is *My Life and Loves* by Frank Harris. In that, the sexual encounters have an eventually wearying sameness whereas, in Lawrence's novel, the progress of Connie's relationship with her husband's gamekeeper is carefully tracked, and there are moments when the sex leaves her relatively indifferent, or she is struck by its ludicrous aspects. As for Millett's further charge that 'Although the male is displayed and admired so often, there is, apart from the word cunt, no reference to or description of the female genitalia: they are hidden, shameful and subject',[37] it could be reasonably objected that the novel provides no justification whatever for the last three words, and that an aroused clitoris or vulva is in any case less immediately visual, and therefore more difficult to describe, than an erect phallus.

Another common charge brought against Mellors is that he has no interest in foreplay. That would be hard to deny in his particular case, or about Lawrence's fiction in general. In many writers the sometimes long road to sexual gratification is what is most interesting whereas at least one of Lawrence's participants in an episode of sexual intercourse tends to be too eager and frustrated to make foreplay possible, and anything that seemed liked deliberate delay would have struck him as titillation. Yet if there is little foreplay in *Lady Chatterley's Lover* there is plenty of play that comes after as is illustrated by the well-known scene in which Mellors and Connie confirm their closeness to Nature by threading flowers into their pubic hair. In an article on the contemporary English novel which T. S. Eliot published in the *Nouvelle Revue Française* in 1927, he complained of Lawrence that when his characters made love, 'or at least accomplish what in Lawrence is the equivalent of love (and they don't do anything else) – not only do they lose all the amenities, refinements and graces which have been elaborated over several centuries to make love bearable, but they seem to reverse the course of evolution and its metamorphoses, regressing beyond the monkey and the fish to some hideous coupling of protoplasm'. There is little doubt Eliot would have felt that the publication of *Lady Chatterley* in 1928 only confirmed what he had to say here. Leaving aside the extraordinary self-betrayal in the reference to making love 'bearable' (*supportable*), which he may have felt he could allow himself because he was writing in French, and the accusation of evolutionary regression, that there is little amenity, refinement and grace in the love-making of Connie and Mellors may be true, depending on one's definition of these three terms; but the idea that it is 'just sex' is clearly wrong, and 'just sex' is a notion with which they, and Lawrence's characters in general, have a great deal of difficulty. They may dream of the dalliance of eagles but find it hard to follow that path. Either sex produces in at least one of them anxiety, anger and revulsion or, as in the case of Mellors and Connie, it generates feelings which it has been customary to describe as love. And, after all, once Connie has become pregnant sex hardly figures, and Mellors's final word at the end of the novel is in praise of chastity. Yet he remains resistant to the idea that while circumstances or even choice curtail their sexual activity, what sustains them in the meantime could be described as love. After their first coming together, Mellors is depressed by all the social complications which are likely to ensue. 'It's just love', Connie tells him cheerfully; to which he replies 'Whatever that may be'. There is a moment during their fourth sexual encounter when Connie is seeking reassurance:

> 'You do love me!', she whispered, assertive. And his hands stroked her softly, as if she were a flower, without the quiver of desire, but with delicate nearness. And still there haunted her a restless necessity to get a grip on love.
>
> 'Say you'll always love me!', she pleaded.
>
> 'Ay!' he said abstractedly. And she felt her questions driving him away from her.[38]

Tenderness and touch ('delicate nearness') are words which Mellors can entertain, but love is one which in him sets alarm bells ringing, and which always threaten to compromise sexual activity, or even the memory of it.

Rooting out shame

The event which did more than any other to make Lawrence an unlikely hero of the frank and open treatment of sex took place thirty years after his death. This was of course the *Lady Chatterley* trial in 1960. Since the witnesses called for the defence were primarily concerned with establishing that the novel could not be called pornographic, their comments had a bias which may have made them different from what they would have been in a more neutral context; but it was nonetheless remarkable that an Anglican bishop could have described Lawrence's novel as a book all Christians should read because it portrayed sex as 'something essentially sacred', and that so many literary authorities should have lined up to praise its merits.[39] Since the general implication was that Lawrence was courageously choosing to discuss activities which are characteristic of most people but which centuries of both formal and informal repression had taught them to keep secret, it was no surprise that the extent to which his particular version of them was by no means what might be called 'normative' began to attract attention. Almost immediately, for example, John Sparrow, the Warden of All Souls, mischievously directed attention to an aspect of the love-making of Mellors and Connie which had not been discussed in the trial. This was during what Lawrence himself calls a 'night of sensual passion' in which Connie was

> a little startled, and almost unwilling: yet pierced again with piercing thrills of sensuality, different, sharper, more terrible than the thrills of tenderness, but, at the moment, more desirable. Though a little frightened, she let him have

his way, and the reckless, shameless sensuality shook her to her foundations.

The experience is one which is said to burn out 'the shames, the deepest, oldest shames, in the most secret places'. The type of shame involved is described as of an organic variety,

> the old, old physical fear which crouches in the bodily roots of us, and can only be chased away by the sensual fire, at last it was roused up and routed by the phallic hunt of the man, and she came to the very heart of the jungle of herself ... But it took some getting at, the core of the physical jungle, the last and deepest recess of organic shame. The phallos alone could explore it. And how he pressed in on her! And how, in fear, she hated it! But how she had really wanted it![40]

For a novel noted for its explicitness, the language here is puzzlingly imprecise. Yet when Mellors's alienated wife, Bertha Coutts, begins to spread rumours about his unusual sexual practices, they hint at anal intercourse and all Lawrence's previous excursions into this territory indicate that Sparrow was right to suggest that this is what is being referred to here.[41] That Connie hates but really likes it is an all too familiar formulation which Millett was one of the first to identify and stigmatise, and it is noteworthy that on the morning after these events Connie says to Mellors, '"I loved last night. But you'll keep the tenderness for me, won't you?"'[42]

The idea of anal intercourse between heterosexuals is not now such a startling idea as it would have been in 1928, or even 1960: since this last date, films such as *Last Tango in Paris* have helped to bring it from the porn industry into the mainstream. Yet that process of habituation is only limited in comparison with the way oral sex is today referred to in the cinema and on television (it might be hard to put together a collection of performances by stand-up comedians, or films for teenagers, in which the expression 'blow-job' is *not* used). That there are no even covert allusions to oral sex in Lawrence's descriptions of the sexual encounters between Connie and the gamekeeper, or of the rumours Bertha Coutts spreads about her husband, may seem surprising. It is true that Mellors is described at one point as gliding his cheek along Connie's belly and kissing the inside of her thigh, but this is without any suggestion of cunnilingus and when she does similar things to him, including kissing his penis, fellatio also seems a long way away.[43] This may be because while in our time oral sex is a widely recognised aspect of some people's sexual practice, in Lawrence's it was very much in the background. Although in Freud's writings it is prominent enough – most people can remember how in the Dora case history he interprets the tickle in his patient's throat as a sign of her desire to indulge in fellatio with her father – it could be there is no oral sex in *Lady Chatterley* because it had never crossed Lawrence's mind that there could or should be. Yet at one moment in the final version he writes that Mellors 'hated mouth kisses'[44] and when, shortly after finishing the first, Lawrence began to take his painting seriously, one of the canvasses he produced was a hideous, satirical representation of two unattractive heads about to engage in the kind of close-up kissing which had shocked him on the few occasions he had been to the cinema.[45] The probability is therefore that, whatever Lawrence's other sexual problems, he was not fixated in what Freudians like to call the oral stage, and that oral sex was not appealing to him.

Anal intercourse is another matter and the question it raises once again is whether Lawrence's interest is an indication of a repressed homosexuality which, the context makes clear, is what Millett is claiming when she takes the 'night of sensual passion' as an acting out of its author's 'own sodomous urges'.[46] My earlier conclusion was that Lawrence was indeed bisexual yet there is not much trace of that in *Lady Chatterley* even if, in the final version, there are details of Mellors's army career which describe how much he loved his colonel, just as his colonel loved him.[47] In all three versions the physique of Connie is described. Although her breasts are periodically celebrated, a major focus is on her buttocks. When early in the final version she is looking at her own body in a mirror and sadly deciding it was going 'dull and opaque' (the same two words that occur in 'Last Words to Miriam'), she concludes that

> the most beautiful part of her was the long-sloping fall of the haunches, from the socket of the back, and the slumberous round stillness of the buttocks. Like hillocks of sand, the Arabs say, soft and down-slipping with a long slope.[48]

Mellors would seem to share this view when, in one of the later love-making scenes, 'he stroked her tail with his hand, long and subtly taking in the curves and the globe-fulness':

> 'Tha's got such a nice tail on thee,' he said, in the throaty, caressive dialect. 'Tha's got the nicest arse of anybody. It's the nicest, nicest woman's arse as is! An' ivry bit of it is woman, woman sure as nuts. Tha'rt not one o' them button-arsed lasses as should be lads, are 'ter. Tha's got a real soft sloping bottom on thee, as a man loves in 'is guts. It's a bottom as could hold the world up, it is.[49]

In one of his paintings, Lawrence offered his own version of the Rape of the Sabine Women and humorously described it as 'a study in arses'. Since all the figures are naked, female buttocks are not the only ones on view but at the centre is a Rubenesque nude whose efforts to escape her captor twist her buttocks round towards the viewer.[50] This feature of the female anatomy definitely attracted Lawrence but whether that is a sure and certain indication of repressed homosexuality must be very doubtful.

Lawrence produced so many paintings in his last years that he was able to arrange an exhibition of them in London. This opened in June 1929 but was very quickly closed down by the authorities. When the police took away several of the exhibits, the criterion for selection appears to have been the depiction on the nudes of pubic hair. Just as, however, when Lawrence had previously suffered from censorship and *The Rainbow* was banned, the motives of the authorities were probably more complicated than they seemed. Officialdom had already been alerted to Lawrence's case by the importation through the ordinary mail of copies of *Lady Chatterley*, mostly but not all destined for private subscribers. When he posted a manuscript of short poems to England it was illegally seized by the British police and the exhibition then gave them a further opportunity which it could be said they had been looking for. One painting which did not appear in it, and which would almost certainly have been confiscated by the police if it had, is called *Le Pisseur*. As the title suggests, this depicts a naked man urinating on the ground with his hand on a nearby wall.[51] To understand why Lawrence chose such an apparently uninteresting subject, and how it relates to the guerrilla war he was waging against censorship, it is useful to go to two paragraphs from his *Pornography and Obscenity* essay, the extended version of which he published in September 1929:

> The sex functions and the excrementary functions in the human body work so close together, yet they are, so to speak, utterly different in direction. Sex is a creative flow, the excrementary flow is towards dissolution, de-creation, if we may use such a word. In the really healthy human being, the distinction between the two is instant, our profoundest instincts are perhaps our instincts of opposition between the two flows.
>
> But in the degraded human being the deep instincts have gone dead, and then the two flows become identical. *This* is the secret of really vulgar people and of pornography: the sex flow and the excrement flow is the same to

them. It happens when the psyche deteriorates, and the profound controlling instincts collapse.[52]

Someone in whom Lawrence felt the collapse of the 'profound controlling instincts' could be clearly seen was Jonathan Swift. In *A Propos of 'Lady Chatterley's Lover'* he suggests that Swift's insanity was at least partly traceable to this cause and instances the poem Swift addressed to his mistress which has 'the maddened refrain: "But Celia, Celia, Celia shits!". Of course Celia shits, Lawrence comments, who doesn't, 'and then think of poor Celia, made to feel iniquitous about her proper natural functions, by the "lover". It is monstrous.'[53]

These remarks provide a context for the moment in *Lady Chatterley* which comes just after Mellors has praised Connie's arse and told her she had got a real sloping bottom on her 'as a man loves in 'is guts':

> All the while he spoke he exquisitely stroked the rounded tail, till it seemed as if a slippery sort of fire came from it into his hand. And his finger tips touched the two secret openings to her body, time after time, with a soft little brush of fire.
>
>   ''An if tha shits an' if tha pisses, I'm glad. I don't want a woman as couldna shit nor piss'. Connie could not help a sudden snirt of astonished laughter, but he went on unmoved. 'Tha'rt real, tha art! Tha'rt real, even a bit of bitch. Here tha' shits and here tha pisses: an' I lay my hand on 'em both, an' I like thee for it. I like thee for it.'[54]

One might think here that the 'really healthy human being' to whom Lawrence refers might not need such an explicit demonstration and that Mellors insists too much. This might throw light on a peculiarity of the 'night of sensual passion' which is not often mentioned. Why, after all, is there so much talk in it of rooting out *shame* and why should shame be so much involved? One explanation could be that Mellors is not proud of those 'sodomous urges' which his preference for anal intercourse reveals. But another, more probable one, is that since the anus is even more likely to be associated with an excrementary function than the penis, he is here facing down his demons and that the intercourse to which he subjects Connie is partly a question of exorcism.

To understand better why exorcism is necessary it is useful to go back to that surprising moment in *Mr. Noon* when Lawrence says that Johanna had 'far more sensual satisfaction' from her husband Everard, who is an easily recognisable portrait of Ernest Weekley, than she is getting from Gilbert Noon. The trouble was, however, that although Everard was 'darkly, furiously sensual', he insisted that this side of his nature should be hidden, only revealing himself at night and being openly 'all for the non-existence of such things'. This is why he calls Johanna 'his snowflower, his white snowflower' and likes to think of her as 'an eternal white virgin whom he was almost violating'. The illustration Lawrence offers of this aspect of Everard is that a W.C. was a place that 'must not exist for him, in this world'. He then describes an occasion when Everard was busy in there and Johanna, 'in her reckless un-English way' and wanting also to use the facility, seized the door handle and, when it would not open, rattled it fiercely. When Everard finally emerges, 'handsome and white with rage, trembling with fury', he asks her with a snarl whether she is mad. Lawrence's conclusion is that 'we've got to start afresh, and laugh at the W.C., and give reverence and honourable fear to the passional sensual fulfilment'.[55] His point is presumably that we need to be open and accepting about *all* the body's functions although quite why inserting the penis in the anus helps to promote that openness and acceptance is not clear, nor is it transparent why (to echo the passage at the beginning of this section) it is the phallus alone which is capable of rooting out shame. Like the privileging of the 'cocygeal' as the most important of the lower body centres, this looks suspiciously like bogus theoretical justification for a sexual practice Lawrence was otherwise inclined to feel uncomfortable about.

BERTHA COUTTS

There is an implication in *Lady Chatterley's Lover* that Mellors's desire to root out shame is for Connie's benefit whereas, for many readers, it feels much more like it is for his. Certainly there appear to be more demons in the gamekeeper's past life than hers. One of them is described in the novel's second version but then disappears from the last. It concerns Parkin's history with Bertha Coutts and Connie's puzzlement as to how he came to marry such a woman. It turns out that when he was eleven or twelve, he had gone to the Coutts's home and found the sixteen year old Bertha on her own. She had lifted up her skirts – 'They wore them split drawers then, girls did' – and shown him her genitals:

> She wanted me to come an' feel. But I never knowed afore then, as women had hair there. Black hair! An' I don't know why, it upset me an' made me hate the thoughts of women from that day.

From this moment on, Parkin says, he remained a virgin and although he and Bertha did nevertheless marry, he found he was unable to make love to her. When he was eventually persuaded to explain to his wife where the trouble lay, Bertha cried all night but then invited Parkin to shave off her pubic hair. "'An so I did, an' she laid there so still. An' then it came up in me, an' I wanted her'".[56]

It may be that Lawrence was experimenting here with a wholly fictitious episode, perhaps based on rumours he had heard of why Ruskin had failed to consummate his marriage with Effie Gray (that the problem was pubic hair was only suggested in print long after the appearance of *Lady Chatterley's Lover*). But the unlikelihood of that is increased by a story George Neville tells in his memoir. He writes of the period when Lawrence, who in his youth was always drawing or painting, 'turned his attention to the female form'. The faces he began with (Neville reports) were always of women with 'incipient moustaches' and this allowed Neville to tease Lawrence about his fondness for Louie Burrows, the woman whom Lawrence was to describe as 'swarthy',[57] once he had become engaged to her (although Jessie Chambers was also on the dark side). From faces Lawrence apparently proceeded to 'busts, back views of the nude etc., and then to whole figures'. Neville describes how he called on Lawrence one evening and found him examining critically the sketch of a female nude he had just finished. Asking whether his friend intended this to be 'a real woman or just a statue', he took the pencil from Lawrence's hand and 'dashed in the shadings under the armpits and on the body'. When Lawrence asked what these were for, Neville replied that it was 'just the difference between your living, breathing woman, full of life and the statue I mentioned. That's HAIR!' According to him, Lawrence response to this information was suddenly and frantically violent. He leapt from his chair and began pummelling his more athletic companion, calling him a 'dirty little devil' and insisting three times that what he said could not be true. 'Course it's true', Neville insisted, 'and more than ever true in a case like that one – a woman who's got Nature enough in her to grow a little moustache'. But Lawrence refused to believe him.[58]

A conventional Freudian way of reading the young Parkin's dismay at the sight of Bertha's pudenda might be to attribute it to castration anxiety. But that is difficult to apply to the Neville episode and there is a more straightforward reading which explains both his account and the references in *Lady Chatterley's* second version. In the first chapter of Zola's *Nana*, when his heroine appears naked on the stage, we are told that it was the golden hairs under her arms, as well as the plump white thighs, which so excited her male public.[59] What Neville appears to have been doing was lifting the erotic appeal of body hair out of a semi pornographic context and displaying it as a wholesome, 'natural' feature of sexual attraction. As a man of the world he wants to teach his inexperienced friend the real meaning and promise of Louie Burrow's slight moustache. He is attacking that idealisation of women which determined that the representation of their naked bodies, in statuary especially, should be smooth and glossy. But if hair can excite, it can also disgust, however much a part of what Neville calls Nature it may be ('*La femme est* naturelle, *c'est-à-dire abominable*', Baudelaire famously wrote).[60] It seems that Lawrence was originally shocked by the idea of female body hair because it indicated that women did not after all operate in a higher, ethereal sphere but on the same, so often unsatisfactory level of natural functioning as men. The alarm which is present in his response would certainly therefore not be one triggered by fear of castration but a result of having to come to terms so suddenly with an idea of a woman with as much animal nature as himself, or rather, since Neville presents him as physically unsure and timid, with possibly much more.[61]

Parkin exhibits a phobia of which there are very few signs in Lawrence's biography. Yet in the second half of *Mr. Noon*, when he is remembering the trip he and Frieda took across the Alps into Italy in 1912, there is a passage which might make one wonder:

> The valley began to depress him. The great slopes shelving upwards, far overhead; the sudden dark, hairy ravines in which he was trapped: all made him feel he was caught, shut in down below there. He felt tiny, like a dwarf among the great thighs and ravines of the mountains. There is a Baudelaire poem which tells of Nature, like a vast woman lying spread, and man, a tiny insect, creeping between her knees and under her thighs, fascinated. Gilbert felt a powerful revulsion against the great slopes and particularly against the tree-dark, hairy ravines in which he was caught.[62]

The reference is to *La Géante* which Lawrence reads far more in accordance with his own preoccupations with 'hairy ravines' than Baudelaire's. It can be associated with a phrase in a letter he had written to Ernest Weekley, a few months before the Alpine excursion: 'All women in their natures are like giantesses'.[63] The aspect of their bodies which Neville claims disturbed Lawrence he clearly got used to, but one can understand why the Connie of *Lady Chatterley's* second version should enquire anxiously of Parkin, 'You don't think the hair on my body is nasty, do you? You don't wish it wasn't there?', and that the gamekeeper should be described as kissing it. If this is also a rite of exorcism then so too are the moments in the final two versions in which the two lovers thread flowers through each other's pubic hair.[64]

The number of demons that can be traced back to Lawrence himself may make him an unlikely hero of sexual liberation, but not the openness with which he is willing to confront them. As Parkin becomes Mellors in the transition from the second to the final versions of the novel, he loses his pubic hair phobia; yet at the same time he acquires a sexual past which is in many respects painfully recognisable as Lawrence's own. There are several other changes which bring him much nearer to his creator. In the final version, for example, his health is frail and he has both a weak chest and a cough. Having crossed the class barrier through education, and his time in the army, his greater degree of articulacy means that he is able to reinforce with his own remarks the authorial criticism of industrialisation. That is now a prominent feature of the novel so that when F. R. Leavis wrote about *Lady Chatterley's Lover* in 1930, a bold move for an academic in that period, he was able to focus on this aspect and say next to nothing about its dealings with sex. Yet on sex also Mellors is articulate, saying many things which one can find echoed in Lawrence's essays. Parkin is a figure distanced from his creator but there are many moments in *Lady Chatterley's Lover* when Mellors and Lawrence appear virtually indistinguishable.

One of these is, as I have said, the gamekeeper's account of the women he has known in the past. When he begins to talk about 'the first girl I began with when I was sixteen', the model is quite clearly Jessie Chambers.

> She was a schoolmaster's daughter over at Ollerton – pretty, beautiful really. I was a supposed-to-be clever sort of young fellow from Sheffield Grammar School, with a bit of French and German, very much up aloft. She was the romantic sort that hated commonness. She egged me on to poetry and reading: in a way, she made a man of me. I read and I thought like a house on fire, for her. And I was a clerk in Butterley Offices, thin, white-faced fellow fuming with all the things I read. And about *everything* I talked to her, but everything. We talked ourselves into Persepolis and Timbuctoo. We were the most literary-cultured couple in ten counties. I held forth with rapture to her, positively with rapture. I simply went up in smoke. And she adored me. – The serpent in the grass was sex. She somehow didn't have any – at least, not where it's supposed to be. I got thinner and crazier. Then I said we'd got to be lovers. I talked her into it, as usual. So she let me. I was excited, and she never wanted it. She just didn't want it. She adored me, and she loved me to talk to her and kiss her: in that way, she had a passion for me. But the other, she just didn't want. And there are lots of women like her. And it was just the other that I *did* want. So there we split. I was cruel and left her.[65]

Apart from a few transpositions: schoolmaster's daughter, Sheffield rather than Nottingham grammar school, the Butterley Offices …, this could well serve as Lawrence's unsympathetic synopsis of the central interest of the chapter of *Sons and Lovers* entitled 'The Test on Miriam'. The fact that it does so clearly refer to Lawrence's own relationship with Jessie Chambers makes what follows immediately a little surprising. That is the account of the next girl Mellors 'took on with': 'a teacher, who had made a scandal by carrying on with a married man and driving him nearly out of his mind'. Here the reference is equally clearly to Helen Corke, that school-teaching colleague of Lawrence's whose account of her affair with a married man – who committed suicide after being driven 'nearly out of his mind' – formed the basis of *The Trespasser*. The surprising detail is that since this woman was 'clinging, caressing, creeping into [him] in every way', Mellors forced her to have sex with him, whereupon, because she 'loved everything about love, except the sex', 'she just ground her teeth and sent out hate'.[66] Now there is no clear evidence that Lawrence did in fact sleep with Helen Corke, although he certainly tried hard enough to do so; but there is some that, although she may have been bisexual, her strongest preference was for relationships with women, or ones with either gender which were intimate but without any sex at all. Whatever the truth, it may help to explain a vicious outburst against lesbians which comes only a little later in Mellors's account, and is one of the many elements which makes the third version of *Lady Chatterley* a harsher and far more bitter work than the first ever was. There are women, Mellors tells Connie,

> that puts you out before you really 'come', and go on writhing their loins till they bring themselves off against your thighs. But they're mostly the Lesbian sort. It's astonishing how Lesbian women are, consciously or unconsciously. Seems to me they're nearly all Lesbian.'
>
> 'And do you mind?', asked Connie.
>
> 'I could kill them. When I'm with a woman who's really Lesbian, I fairly howl in my soul, wanting to kill her.'
> …
>
> 'But do you think Lesbian women any worse than homosexual men?'
>
> '*I* do! Because I've suffered more from them'[67]

These remarks may remind many readers how the tone in the account of Ursula's brief affair with her schoolmistress in *The Rainbow* begins sympathetically but then suddenly turns harsh and condemnatory, and make them wonder why Lawrence's gradual if reluctant acceptance of active homosexuality in men was not matched by a similar development as far as women were concerned, although there is one, hardly satisfactory, answer to that question here in Mellors's 'because I've suffered more from them'.

The angry and intemperate tone of the passage above is very much in evidence as Mellors describes his marriage to Bertha Coutts. He explains that the relationship with her had coincided with his decision to leave the 'Butterley Offices' and become a blacksmith, as well as to adopt the dialect in preference to standard English, although 'I still read books, at home'. Bertha he liked because 'she wanted me, and made no bones about it. And I was pleased as punch. That was what I wanted: a woman who *wanted* me to fuck her'. Yet being as pleased as punch, and 'bringing her breakfast in bed sometimes', made Bertha despise him a little so that,

> she got so's she'd never have me when I wanted her: never. Always put me off, …But when I had her, she'd never come off when I did. Never! She'd just wait. If I kept back for half an hour, she'd keep back longer. And when I'd come and really finished, then she'd start on her own account, and I had to stop inside her till she'd brought herself off, wriggling and shouting. And when I'd gone little as anything, she'd clutch clutch clutch with herself down there, an' then she'd come off, fair in ecstasy. An' then she'd say: That was lovely!

A further problem was that Bertha became harder and harder to 'bring off', and 'she'd sort of tear at me down there, as if it was a beak tearing at me'

By God, you think a woman's soft down there, like a fig. But I tell you the old rampers have beaks between their legs, and they tear at you with it till you're sick. Self! self! self! all self! tearing and shouting! They talk about men's sensual selfishness, but I doubt whether it can ever touch a woman's blind beakishness, once she's gone that way. Like an old trull! And she couldn't help it. I told her about it, I told her how I hated it. And she'd even try. She'd try to lie still and let *me* work the business. She'd try. But it was no good. She got no feeling off it, from my working. She had to work the thing herself, grind her own coffee. And it came back on her like a raving necessity, she had to let herself go, and tear, tear, tear, as if she had no sensation in her except in the top of her beak, the very outside top tip, that rubbed and tore.[68]

When witnesses in the *Lady Chatterley* trial talked about how reverently and beautifully sexual intercourse can be represented by Lawrence, they did well to ignore this passage. The complaints in it are very similar to those made about Kate in *The Plumed Serpent*, but they are even more virulently expressed: here more obviously is what has been termed the *vagina dentata*. In initial physical descriptions the Connie Chatterley of *Lady Chatterley's Lover* may owe most to Rosalind Baynes (whose sculptor father was an actual member of the Royal Academy, as Connie's is described as being); but as the character develops through the novel, she acquires many of Frieda's attributes and, in later life, Frieda certainly showed no tendency to contradict those who identified Connie with her. Yet if many aspects of the novel's heroine are reminiscent of Frieda at her uninhibited best (running naked in the rain, for example), Bertha Coutts must surely often represent for Lawrence what was his wife's dark side. Where else but from his relations with Frieda, and in a context which is so manifestly autobiographical, could he have accumulated such a reserve of intense sexual distaste? Certainly the

language here might make one hesitate to assume that the impotence which there is good evidence to attribute to Lawrence in his last years can be entirely a matter of failing health.

That Connie was also in the habit of 'holding back' is one of the new elements added to the final version of Lawrence's novel. In that she has been sent to Dresden in her teens and found there a German lover, all too anxious for the 'love-connection'. 'But a woman could yield to a man without yielding her inner, free self':

> For she had only to hold herself back, in the sexual intercourse, and let him finish and expend himself without herself coming to the crisis; and then she could prolong the connection and achieve her orgasm and crisis while he was merely a tool.[69]

This is precisely what so angers Mellors about Bertha, but Connie's behaviour is not the same when she is with him. Sometimes, it is true, she is an indifferent spectator to what is going on and finds the movement of his buttocks ridiculous; but that does not prompt her to take charge of the situation. There is one moment of mutual orgasm on which Mellors comments (his tendency to give Connie mini-lectures on sexuality being a new feature of version three), but mostly she can rely on his ability to 'come and come again' so that if she waits long enough there is a strong likelihood of her finding what is referred to in relation to Kate as her 'satisfaction'. Unlike Bertha therefore, she is willing to lie still and let *him* work the business. In his theoretical writing especially, Lawrence's fierce dualism means that he always tends to see things in terms of opposites. In sexual intercourse there is for him an inevitable power struggle which means that either the woman or the man must come out on top. When Millett complains, therefore, that the scenes of sexual intercourse in the novel – and she means of course those between Mellors and Connie – are written according to a 'female is passive, male is active' formula, she is broadly right. This is whatever one thinks of her then attributing this formula to Freud[70] and ignoring Lawrence's implicit claim that passivity can also lead to satisfaction.

Between her young German lover and Mellors, Connie also has an affair in the novel's final version with a highly successful playwright called Michaelis. The way in which he is represented has a lot to do with Lawrence having met in Florence a man he had known during the war years as Dikran Kouyoumdjian. Since that time, this writer of Armenian extraction had wisely changed his name to Michael Arlen and become rich and famous as the author of one of the most spectacular best-sellers of the 1920s, *The Green Hat*. In her sexual encounters with Michaelis Connie carries on when he has finished, but that is because he is portrayed as such an inadequate lover: at one point there is a reference to his 'pathetic two-second spasms'. 'Like so many modern men', Connie reflects, '[Michaelis] was finished almost before he had begun',[71] and she is clearly grateful that Mellors is not 'modern' in this sense. One of the more unappealing aspects of *Lady Chatterley's Lover,* which is even more prominent when Lawrence comes to defend the novel in *A Propos*, is this assumption that most, if not all, modern young men are sexually inadequate. It was of course foolish of the British authorities to seek to continue the ban on the novel, but if they had wanted to make a stronger case they might well have pointed less to its potentially corrupting effect on young women, and more to how discouraging it might prove for nervous, uncertain young men.

CHAPTER SIX:
A PROPOS

In *A Propos of 'Lady Chatterley's Lover'*, the bodies of both men and women are described as having become like trained dogs, with everything reflected downwards from the mind. This means that 'love is a counterfeit feeling today'[1] and sex, however much more widely indulged, counterfeit also. With rare exceptions, everyone is like Clifford in being 'out of touch', or like Yvette in *The Virgin and the Gipsy* and Connie in *Lady Chatterley's Lover*, both of whom are initially described in terms of the Lady of Shallot whose contacts with reality are through reflections in a mirror. How to know that one was dealing with a real world was a question which had preoccupied Lawrence from early in his career, and he took it up again when he had to write an introduction for a book in which many of his paintings were being reproduced. Wondering then how the division between mental and intuitive consciousness came about, he notes the difference between Chaucer and Shakespeare, and conjectures that the morbid fear of the body, which he claims is so prevalent in the writings of the latter, might have been due to the sudden impact of syphilis on the Western mind generally. This would have spread a fear which he believes has never gone away, one that has a particularly devastating effect on the pictorial arts because they depend so much 'on the intuitional perception of the *reality* of substantial bodies'. In English eighteenth-century portrait painting, he suggests, all the concentration is on the clothes the subjects wear rather than the people in them, and the *ne plus ultra* of the escape from reality comes in French Impressionism 'when the body was at last dissolved of its substance, and made part and parcel of the sunlight-and-shadow scheme'. This is what, in Lawrence's view, makes Cézanne such an important figure. Roger Fry had claimed that when Cézanne retired from Paris back to his native Provence, it was so that he could give himself up entirely to a 'desperate search for the reality hidden beneath the veil', and he had stressed the painter's interest in the geometry of composition: that aspect of his work which helped to give rise to Cubism.[2] Lawrence had a low opinion of Cézanne's successors, comparing them to Chinese dressmakers who reproduce in exact replica the darned rent in the Western dresses they are copying. For him, Cézanne was not searching for anything beyond or behind what was there but 'true-to-life representation. Only he wanted it *more* true to life'. His own painting he places in this same tradition of Cézanne's, trying to connect with the world as it actually is. He correctly identifies in Fry a lurking Platonism: the influence of that 'arch priest of the crucifixion of the body in favour of the spirit'. But that raises the question of quite when the move away from substance and the body could be said to have begun, given his claim that between Chaucer and Shakespeare there occurred a radical change. His answer lies in saying that 'the Renaissance put the spear through the side of the *already crucified* body, and syphilis put poison in the wound made by the imaginative spear' (my italics).[3]

In *A Propos*, Plato's responsibility for having established the rule of spirit, of initiating the 'idealist epoch', is shared with Jesus and the Buddha who are accused of not only bringing idealism into the world but also tragedy since 'they were all three utter pessimists as regards life'. But this insistence on the triumph of the mind over the body, so that the body is its tool and everything is 'reflected downwards' from it, can make the opening of Lawrence's essay disconcerting. There he defends the use of words like cunt, fuck, shit and piss by not only saying that they are a 'natural part of the mind's consciousness of the body', but also that what he wants to achieve by using them is that men and women should to be able 'to *think* sex, fully, completely, honestly, and cleanly'. This is because 'ours is the day of realisation rather than action', and 'only fresh mental realisation will freshen up the experience'.[4] How this freshening up is to be differentiated from that use of the mind for directing the body he elsewhere denounces is no clearer than how the words in question should be able to perform that function. He seems to feel that fuck, cunt, shit and piss are part of our natural consciousness because they have an Anglo-Saxon origin and were more commonly used by the working than middle or upper classes of his day for, after all, 'the working classes retain the old blood-warmth of oneness and togetherness' longer than those higher up the social scale. But the origins or currency of words are nothing in comparison with *how* they are used and though fuck (for example) is now far more often pronounced in public than in Lawrence's time that does not mean that its users have more reverence for what it signifies. Quite the contrary, in fact. Lawrence's four-letter words may or may not have been preferable to the alternatives, but they had (and have) been used for so long, and so regularly, in hostile and demeaning contexts, that his hope of being able to recuperate them through the influence of a single book always seemed forlorn.

The precise manner in which the 'so-called obscene words' are defended in *A Propos* is not its only disconcerting feature. Arguing against George Bernard Shaw who had criticised the Pope for protesting against a modern trend in women to cover themselves up less, and suggested that if one really wanted advice on the relation between clothes and sex-appeal it would be much better to consult, not Europe's Chief Priest, but its Chief Prostitute (supposing such a person to exist), Lawrence contends that the ignorance prostitutes have of 'real sex' comes from their awareness of their inability to attach men to them permanently and their 'rage against the profound instinct of fidelity in a man'. Although one would have thought that prostitutes, of all women, not only accepted but positively welcomed and required that their relations with men should be temporary, Lawrence says further that the real sex the prostitute can never know is a matter of 'the rhythm of the seasons and the years'. He is then led on to a defence of the Catholic Church since, whereas Protestantism brought an emphasis on the individual rather than the community, Catholicism (he feels) had always seen, and to some degree continued to see, the individual life as embedded in the rituals of the year and the seasons. What a catastrophe it was, he observes, when people were cut off from these. In his opinion Catholicism was and is established on 'the element of *union* in mankind', the first example of which is the marriage tie so that 'The Church really rests upon the indissolubility of marriage'. In spite of discussing a novel in which the principal action is adultery, Lawrence expresses his approval of this indissolubility although he recognises that, because 'there is no marriage apart from the wheeling sun and the nodding earth', the partners in a marriage are themselves always changing. But this is as it should be given that 'the changing harmony and discord of [the variation of men and women] make the secret music of life'.

> And is not so throughout life? A man is different at thirty, at forty, at fifty, at sixty, at seventy: and the woman at his side is different. But is there not some strange conjunction in their differences? Is there not some peculiar harmony, through youth, the period of childbirth, the period of florescence and young children, the period of the woman's change of life, painful yet also a renewal, the period of waning passion but mellowing delight of affection, the dim unequal period of the approach of death, when the man and woman look at one another with the dim apprehension of separation that is not really a separation: is there not, throughout it all, some unseen, unknown interplay of balance, harmony, completion, like some soundless symphony which moves with a rhythm from phase to phase, so different, so very different in the various movements, and yet one symphony, made out of the soundless singing of two strange and incompatible lives, a man's and a woman's?[5]

In so many of his beliefs and attitudes (including his conviction that all genuine passion is sacred) Lawrence is one of the last great Romantics; but he only occasionally writes as romantically as he does here where the unspoken topic might be reasonably described as the enduring and yet ever changing nature of love. Another way of characterising this passage would be to say that here Lawrence is elaborating eloquently on Clifford's claim, previously quoted, that in marriage 'little by little, living together, two people fall into a sort of unison, they vibrate so intricately to one another'. As if aware of this danger, and that his vision of marriage as a sound-less symphony could begin to suggest that his own predominant tune was beginning to change, Lawrence puts himself into reverse with a crucial qualification. 'But –', he writes 'and this *but* crashes through the heart like a bullet –marriage is not marriage which is not basically and permanently phallic'. The word phallic, rather than the 'sexual' which would be equally appropriate in this con-text, is often in Lawrence a signal for a wider meaning. Just as Freud will occasionally use 'sex' to refer to the ubiquitous presence of powerful instinctual drives, rather than to copulation, so the 'phallic consciousness' is sometimes used by Lawrence to indicate a relationship with the natural world which is physical and emo-tional (intuitive) rather than mental. Yet here he leaves his reader in no doubt that it is the narrower meaning he has in mind. Early in his career he had declared that 'my great religion is a belief in the blood'[6] and in this essay, written near the end of it, he returns to at least one aspect of this position by describing true marriage as a 'correspondence of blood'.

> The blood of man and the blood of woman are two eter-nally different streams, that can never be mingled. Even scientifically we know it. But therefore they are the two rivers that encircle the whole of life, and in marriage the circle is complete, and in sex the two rivers touch and re-new one another, without ever commingling or confusing.

We know it. The phallus is a column of blood, that fills the valley of blood of a woman. The great river of male blood touches to its depth the great river of female blood, yet neither breaks its bounds. It is the deepest of all communions, as all the religions, *in practice*, know. And it is one of the greatest mysteries: in fact, the greatest, as almost every apocalypse shows, showing the supreme achievement of the mystic marriage.[7]

The appearance of the word mystic here is a warning signal. It takes one back to all the reading in Theosophy, and kindred areas, which Lawrence had done in the first years of the war and to the habit, so pronounced in *Fantasia of the Unconscious*, to claim for the most outlandish propositions the status of scientific fact. What genuine science there is to confirm that the blood of men and women can never be co-mingled (in a blood transfusion, for example) would be hard to say, but the claim does articulate once again the familiar problem in Lawrence of how, in a relation so intimate as sexual intercourse, the two parties can retain their individuality. It also, with the reference to 'the two rivers that encircle the whole of life', puts sex firmly back at the centre of things. How little room that might therefore leave for what is implied in the 'mellowing delight of affection' of those couples in whom passion is waning, for example, is emphasised as Lawrence goes on to claim that 'affinity of mind and personality is an excellent basis for friendship between the sexes, but a disastrous basis for marriage'. The reason for this is that 'the sympathy of nerves and mind and personal interest is, alas, hostile to blood-sympathy, in the sexes'.[8]

Schopenhauer had suggested that there was no necessary coincidence between whatever makes one person sexually attractive to another and their personal qualities, so that the result of society's attempt to confine sex to marriage is often disastrous. Lawrence goes further here and suggests that sex and 'personal interest' are in absolute contradiction (he is perhaps thinking back to his relationship with Jessie Chambers). This is hard to reconcile with his charming evocation of the way a marriage evolves over time, and moreover if such a marriage needs to be not only basically phallic (like Mrs. Bolton's) but permanently so (which Lawrence's own certainly wasn't), then the belief he appears to have sustained for most of his adult life that love must always be 'free' may have to be ditched overboard also. There is in any case little room for compromise between a belief in free love and a conviction that marriage should be indissoluble, unless one accepts that a marriage which is free, or in the more usual terminology 'open', is just as much a marriage as any other. But that is a position which is hardly ever been in favour with the Catholic Church.

How love and sex can be related is a question which had troubled Lawrence from the start. Here, at the end of his life and career, he is as confused and contradictory as he ever was on the issue. This hardly puts him in a strong position to lecture the young on sexual matters, as he so often does, and nor did it make him the ideal spokesman in the 1960s for sexual liberation. After he had finished *Sons and Lovers*, Lawrence told Garnett that it was 'the tragedy of thousands of young men in England – it may even be Bunny's tragedy. I think it was Ruskin's, and men like him.'9 Given that Freud had only recently published an essay in which he talked about how many men there were whose sex lives were ruined or distorted by an excessive devotion to their mothers or sisters, there seems to have been some justification for this claim to representativeness. But that Lawrence's experiences of sex after his meeting with Frieda could ever be called representative seems improbable. To have authority and dispense useful advice on sex requires an understanding of one's own feelings and those of others. It is not clear that Lawrence was sufficiently aware of how unusual he was to be the first person a young person should approach for the resolution of sexual problems.

Being unrepresentative does not however make a writer who deals with sex less interesting. It could perhaps be claimed that what entitled Lawrence to the position he sometimes attained in the 1960s is not the clarity and coherence of what he has to say, but the extraordinary willingness he always displayed to expose himself to his readers, and work away at his difficulties in the public forum of poetry and prose. 'You were a man of destiny, driven to sacrifice yourself in order that men might know themselves', as Murry once grandiloquently put it.[10] Yet a major qualification for this role is perhaps that 'terrifying honesty' which F. R. Leavis once attributed to both him and Blake,[11] and there is reason to doubt whether Lawrence always has this attribute when it comes to questions of love and sex. The numerous portrayals of super-potent men who overpower their women with their sexual prowess, for example, smack of wish-fulfilment; and there are suggestions of evasive rationalisation in his descriptions of the physical appeal which one man might have for another and a lack of honesty in the way he dealt with his own attraction to the bodies of men. His first rule was the denial of all repression, but he avoided the many difficulties of this position by making a distinction between – to rely on the terms he employs in *A propos* – desires which are counterfeit and real, with only the latter qualifying as holy. How to make that distinction is however not at all clear and there is a suspicion in his own writing that the criteria to which he appeals are sometimes those of emotional convenience.

On his last trip to England in 1926, Lawrence met up with an old friend from Eastwood called Willie Hopkin who had the temerity to ask him why he had not married Jessie Chambers. Lawrence refused to respond for a while but is then reported to have said: 'It would have been a fatal step. I should have had too easy a life, nearly everything my own way, and my genius would have been destroyed'.[12] In the vast majority of cases counter-factual thinking is futile, but in this one there does seem some point in wondering whether Frieda was quite the best thing that ever happened to

Lawrence, as she herself frequently maintained (that she and she alone must have provided the inspiration for the fearsome Bertha Coutts was a conclusion Frieda seems to have ignored, or brushed off as an aberration). The long-repressed explosion of sexual feeling he enjoyed with her – long-repressed in him – was certainly crucial for both his life and writing. Before meeting her, he had already indentified sexuality as a topic which previous British novelists had avoided and determined to make it his main concern. Frieda provided him with qualifications for the job, but whether he would have continued to feel that sex is the key to all mythologies without her, might be doubted. And equally doubtful is whether she was the right woman to deal with all the relatively unusual forms sex took in Lawrence. Yet it was to Frieda he owed his first sexual awakening and, like many of his characters, that had to mean for him that they were bound to each other even when, to echo a popular expression, there was between them very little love lost.

Lawrence's use of the word 'genius' about himself can seem uncomfortable. In the older meaning of the word it refers to no more than a particular or special talent (which is maybe what he meant); its more recent sense has the misfortune of implying the individual identified has abilities which defy rational analysis and can do no wrong. Ford Madox Hueffer was closer to this later meaning when, on the top of a London bus, he told Lawrence that he had genius. 'In the early days', Lawrence comments, 'they were always telling me I had got genius, as if to console me for not having their own incomparable advantages'.[13] What Hueffer and others recognised was that this son of a miner was prodigiously gifted and that this was becoming increasingly evident as his career developed. My topic in this book has obliged me to concentrate on material closely related to his own experience but in fact he was inexhaustibly creative, endlessly fertile in characters and situations and not at all like the William Wordsworth whom Shelley accused of not being able to 'fancy another situation / From which to dart his contemplation, / Than that wherein he stood'.[14] It is a tired commonplace to praise

the presentation of a working-class household in the first part of *Sons and Lovers* but only because, for anyone familiar with the realist tradition in English fiction, no praise could be high enough. How Lawrence moved from there to his next two novels, developing wholly original techniques for what he wanted to say, is an achievement for which it is not at all surprising Frieda wanted to claim some credit. In those books, and many others from roughly the same period, Lawrence became an acute social historian and critic; but also an effective satirist with an acerbic comic touch as well as someone with an uncanny ability to convey those feelings of his characters which lie just below the level of consciousness. And throughout he never lost a talent, unparalleled in modern English writers, to evoke the natural world.

When we look now at Lawrence's last years they seem wholly dominated by *Lady Chatterley's Lover* and Lawrence's battles against censorship. Yet as I have indicated, both *Etruscan Places* and *The Escaped Cock* were published after the novel. Apart from highly effective dramatisations of the everyday problems and encounters which are always part of travel, this first work is also full of vivid evocations of the wall paintings in the Etruscan tombs that he and a male friend visited, and of the surrounding countryside. The last of Lawrence's travel books, it manages to be effective in a different mode from that of its predecessor, *Mornings in Mexico*, a slim volume of sketches which, as far his Mexican or New Mexican experiences are concerned, might well eventually weigh heavier in the critical balance than *The Plumed Serpent*. In *The Escaped Cock* Lawrence is able to evoke a Middle Eastern biblical setting with delicacy and charm and tackle a topic which gave him numerous opportunities for being offensive with great tact. There are strengths in these late books (as there are of course also in the late poetry) which my concentration on love and sex occludes so that it might well appear a pity that his present reputation among the general public makes an effort to set the record straight on those two matters necessary. That I have been able to do so will no doubt be disputed but, in any case, my main aim has been rather to describe as clearly as I can Lawrence's dealings with love and sex so that readers have the opportunity of deciding the issues for themselves. That does not of course mean that I am under the illusion of having been able to describe his case 'objectively' (my very use here of 'case', which I intend to be neutral, might confirm for some how impossible that is); yet I have tried to put enough material on view for people to make as many of the adjustments of emphasis and perspective they might think necessary. Lawrence was a great writer but the relative lack of critical attention he has received recently means that there has been insufficient effort to define more precisely what that ex-pression really means. That can only be done, it seems to me, once his dealings with love and sex have been made clear.

Notes

Preface

1. G. H. Neville, *A Memoir of D. H. Lawrence ('The Betrayal')*, ed. Carl Baron (Cambridge University Press, 1981), p. 78.
2. *The Letters of D. H. Lawrence*, vol. 1, ed. James T. Boulton (Cambridge University Press, 1979), p. 493.
3. *Writing the Body in D. H. Lawrence. Essays on Language, Representation and Sexuality*, ed. Paul Poplawski (Westport: Greenwood Press, 2001), p. ix.
4. See D. H. Lawrence, *The 'Study of Thomas Hardy' and Other Essays*, ed. Bruce Steele (Cambridge University Press, 1985), p. 209.
5. See Lawrence's 'A Propos of *Lady Chatterley's Lover'* in Michael Squires's edition of *Lady Chatterley's Lover* (Cambridge University Press, 1993), p. 309.
6. An almost solitary exception to the absence of monographs on Lawrence to appear in England recently is John Beer's *D. H. Lawrence: Nature, Narrative, Art, Identity* (Palgrave, 2014). This illustrates with almost embarrassing clarity that effect of the writings of F. R. Leavis to which I refer earlier in this preface. Leavis is the critic most frequently cited in Beer's text, in which there is very little about love, and even less about sex. Why this matters becomes clear on p. 188 when he is discussing the first version of *Lady Chatterley's Lover*. This work culminates, Beer writes, 'in Constance's recognition that she must choose between Parkin, with whom she has fallen in love, but who shows little awareness of books or the life of the mind, and a husband who does not care for her, despite being thoughtful and full of interesting conversation.' Whether or not it is fair to say that Clifford *does not care* for his wife, it should be obvious that these words disguise what it has now become fashionable to call an elephant in the room. I don't myself understand how one can talk about *Lady Chatterley's Lover* sensibly, in any of the versions, without fully acknowledging its presence.
7. These are Johnson's final words in *Rambler 60 ('Dignity and Uses of Biography')*, widely available in many different editions.
8. The introduction can be found in D. H. Lawrence, *Introductions and Reviews*, eds. N. H. Reeve and John Worthen (Cambridge University Press, 2005), p. 70.

Chapter 1

1. *Lady Chatterley's Lover* (Cambridge University Press, 1993), p. 200.
2. *Essays of Schopenhauer*, translated by Mrs. Rudolf Dircks (London: Scott Library Ltd., 1897), p. 171.
3. Ibid., p. 172.

4. Ibid., p. 168.
5. Ibid., pp. 192, 187, 190.
6. Jessie Chambers, *D. H. Lawrence: A Personal Record* (Cambridge University Press, 1980), p. 111.
7. *Essays of Schopenhauer*, p. 179.
8. *A Personal Record*, p. 111.
9. Ibid., p. 139. There is no reason to doubt the accuracy of Jessie Chambers's reporting here, especially as many of the words she records are repeated in Lawrence's dramatisation of the episode in *Sons and Lovers*, eds. Helen Baron and Carl Baron (Cambridge University Press, 1992), pp. 261–5, although there is always the possibility that, in looking back, Jessie was remembering the novel as much as the episode itself.
10. *Letters*, vol. 1, p. 141.
11. See M. Kinkead-Weekes, *D. H. Lawrence: Triumph to Exile* (Cambridge University Press, 1996), p. 551.
12. *Letters*, vol. 1, p. 65.
13. *A Personal Record*, p. 117.
14. D. H. Lawrence, *The White Peacock*, ed. Andrew Robertson (Cambridge University Press, 1983), pp. 222–3.
15. Ibid., pp. 366 (note on 66:1), 87.
16. Neville, *A Memoir of D. H. Lawrence*, pp. 79, 95.
17. See *Selected Letters of E. M. Forster* vol. 1, eds. M. Lago and P. N. Furbank (London: Collins, 1983), p. 222.
18. Stendhal, *De l'amour*, ed. Xavier Bourdenet (Paris: Folio, 2014), p. 62 (my translation). For Lawrence's knowledge of the book see the checklist of Lawrence's reading by Rose Marie Burwell in *A D. H. Lawrence Handbook*, ed. Keith Sagar (Manchester University Press, 1982), p. 86. There is no record of what Lawrence thought of it.
19. *The 'Study of Thomas Hardy' and Other Essays*, p. 115.
20. D. H. Lawrence, *Amores* (London: Duckworth, 1916), pp. 10–11.
21. *Letters*, vol. 1, p. 353.
22. See *Scrutiny*, vol. 1, p. 273 (December 1932) and *D. H. Lawrence: Novelist* (London: Chatto and Windus, 1955), p. xiii.
23. See *Introductions and Reviews*, pp. 207–12.
24. D. H. Lawrence, '*Psychoanalysis and the Unconscious*' and '*Fantasia of the Unconscious*', ed. Bruce Steele (Cambridge University Press, 2004), p. 139.
25. See D. H. Lawrence, *Late Essays and Articles*, ed. James T. Boulton (Cambridge University Press, 2004), pp. 245–6.
26. *Love Among the Haystacks and Other Stories*, ed. John Worthen (Cambridge University Press, 1987), p. 105.
27. *Letters*, vol. 1, p. 157.
28. D. H. Lawrence, *The Trespasser*, ed. Elizabeth Mansfield (Cambridge University Press, 1981), p. 134.

29. D. H. Lawrence, *The Poems*, ed. Christopher Pollnitz (Cambridge University Press, 2013), vol. 1, pp. 23–4. It is interesting that in *Sons and Lovers* Paul blames Miriam for developing an anthropomorphic approach to Nature in him: 'Anthropomorphic as she was, she stimulated him into appreciating things thus …' (p. 179).

30. D. H. Lawrence, *Look! We Have Come Through!* (London: Chatto and Windus, 1917), pp. 126, 131.

31. D. H. Lawrence, *The Rainbow*, ed. Mark Kinkead-Weekes (Cambridge University Press, 1989), p. 20.

32. Ibid.

33. See vol. 7 in the Pelican Freud Library, *On Sexuality*, ed. Angela Richards (1977), pp. 245–60.

34. Neville, *A Memoir of D. H. Lawrence*, p. 86.

35. D. H. Lawrence, *Sons and Lovers*, p. 333.

36. Ibid., p. 341.

37. *Amores*, pp. 42–3.

38. *The White Peacock*, p. 307. This reference occurs at a point where Emily has been married off to a wholly decent character in a way which would suggest that Lawrence never stopped feeling guilty about Jessie and wanting to see her happy. Yet in the short story 'The Shades of Spring', the feelings of the protagonist (and author) are more complicated. There, that the figure who is unmistakably based on Jessie has formed a satisfactory sexual relationship with the local gamekeeper makes her returning ex-lover, who has become a successful writer, uncomfortable and he has thoughts such as 'And gradually he was realising that she was something quite other, and always had been', as well as 'He knew now it never had been true, that which was between him and her, not for a moment' – see *The Prussian Officer and Other Stories*, ed. John Worthen (Cambridge University Press, 1983), pp. 104, 110. But to investigate this complicated matter of Lawrence's attitude to Jessie further would take me too far from my main theme, especially when, as Eliott Morsia has made clear in a recent number of *The Journal of D. H. Lawrence Studies*, stories like 'The Shades of Spring' were so often revised (vol. 3. no. 3 (2014), pp. 153–78).

39. *The White Peacock*, p. 67.

40. Elizabeth Cleghorn Gaskell, *The Life of Charlotte Bronte* (Everyman edition, 1908), pp. 184–5. This book was first published in 1857 but this would probably be the edition Lawrence knew.

41. See *Letters*, vol. 1, p. 197.

42. Neville, *A Memoir of D. H. Lawrence*, pp. 86–7.

43. *Sons and Lovers*, pp. 350–2, 383.

44. Ibid., p. 398.

45. *Essays of Schopenhauer*, p. 201.

46. *Sons and Lovers*, p. 291.

47. Ibid., p. 399.

48. Ibid., pp. 399, 407.
49. Ibid., p. 408.
50. Ibid., pp. 361–2.

CHAPTER 2

1. See John Worthen, *D. H. Lawrence: The Early Years* (Cambridge University Press, 1991), p. 380.
2. D. H. Lawrence, *Women in Love*, eds. David Farmer, Lindeth Vasey and John Worthen (Cambridge University Press, 1987), p. 15; D. H. Lawrence, *Lady Chatterley's Lover*, p. 66.
3. *The Rainbow*, p. 29.
4. See D. H. Lawrence, *The Prussian Officer and Other Stories*, ed. John Worthen (Cambridge University Press, 1983), p. 86. For the earlier version ('Two Marriages') see pp. 209–46 in this same volume.
5. *Schopenhauer's Essays*, p. 208.
6. *Letters*, vol. 1, p. 392.
7. Ibid., pp. 403, 414, 440, 458.
8. Frieda Lawrence, *'Not I, But the Wind . . . '* (Santa Fe; The Rydal Press, 1934), p. 23.
9. See John Worthen, *D. H. Lawrence: The Early Years*, pp. 443–4.
10. See *Letters*, vol. 1, p. 421.
11. Ibid., p. 477.
12. *'Not I, But the Wind . . . '*, p. 23 and *Letters*, vol. 1, p. 449.
13. See *D. H. Lawrence: A Composite Biography*, ed. Edward Nehls (The University of Wisconsin Press, 1957), vol. 1, p. 215.
14. *Sons and Lovers*, p. 254.
15. *Letters*, vol. 2, eds. George J. Zytaruk and James T. Boulton (Cambridge University Press, 1981), p. 655.
16. D. H. Lawrence, *'Psychoanalysis and the Unconscious'* and *'Fantasia of the Unconscious'*, pp. 11, 12.
17. Ibid, p. 145.
18. 'Hymn to Priapus' is in *Look! We Have Come Through!* (1917), pp. 20–2.
19. See illustration 42 in John Worthen, *The Early Years*.
20. The episode is dealt with well by Mark Kinkead-Weekes in *D. H. Lawrence: Triumph to Exile*, p. 21.
21. The poems about Lawrence's mother which I mention are roughly contemporary with the letter to Rachel Annand Taylor in which he says that he and his mother have loved each other 'almost with a husband and wife love' and that the relationship has made him 'in some respects, abnormal' (*Letters*, vol. 1, p. 190). It is as if, in these poems, he is trying to find an appropriate vocabulary for that abnormality. The strange insistence on his mother's recovered virginity reoccurs as late as 1922 in 'Spirits Summoned West'

which is ostensibly concerned with the death of an old Eastwood friend but includes lines such as: 'Come back, then, mother, my love, whom I told to die / It was only I who saw the virgin you / That had no home'. See David Ellis, *Dying Game* (Cambridge University Press,1998), p. 73.

22. 'New Eve and Old Adam' in *'Love Among the Haystacks' and Other Stories*, p. 164.
23. For the details of this episode, see *D. H. Lawrence: Triumph to Exile*, p. 35.
24. 'New Eve and Old Adam', p. 161.
25. My various quotations from different parts of 'New Eve and Old Adam' can be found between pp. 161–83 of *'Love Among the Haystacks' and Other Stories*.
26. *Look! We Have Come Through!*, p. 10.
27. 'New Eve and Old Adam', p. 164.
28. *Look! We Have Come Through* (1917), pp. 121–4.
29. D. H. Lawrence, *The Rainbow*, ed. Mark Kinkead-Weekes (Cambridge University Press, 1989), pp. 142, 152.
30. Ibid., p. 141.
31. Ibid., p. 151.
32. Ibid., p. 171.
33. Ibid., p. 218.
34. Ibid., p. 220.
35. Mark Kinkead-Weekes, *D. H. Lawrence: Triumph to Exile*, p. 156. The normal interpretation of the remark which Middleton Murry reports would be that Frieda was complaining that Lawrence liked to penetrate her vulva from behind; but everything we know about their relationship points rather to anal intercourse.
36. *Women in Love*, p. 373.
37. See *The Prussian Officer and Other Stories*, pp. 1–21.
38. *Letters*, vol. 2, p. 115.
39. Ibid., pp. 284–5.
40. Ibid., pp. 320–1.
41. Ibid.
42. The 'Prologue' is printed as an appendix to the Cambridge edition of *Women in Love*, pp. 489–506. Compare with the reference to sitting next to young soldiers, the passage from *The Trespasser* quoted on pp. 14–15 above.
43. Ibid., p. 505.
44. See D. H. Lawrence., *'Reflections on the Death of a Porcupine' and other Essays*, ed. Michael Herbert (Cambridge University Press, 1988), pp. 472.
45. 'The Reality of Peace' is also in *'Reflections on the Death of a Porcupine'*. For this quotation see p. 37.
46. Ibid., p. 35.
47. *Letters*, vol. 2, p. 141.
48. In December 1919 Lawrence thought it would be a 'very good idea' if *The Rainbow* could be republished as *Women in Love: Part One*. See *Letters*,

vol. 3, eds. James Boulton and Andrew Robertson (Cambridge University Press, 1984), p. 439.

49. *The Rainbow*, p. 444.
50. Ibid., pp. 444–5.
51. *Women in Love*, p. 345.
52. *Letters*, vol. 1, pp. 406–7.
53. *Women in Love*, p. 345.
54. Ibid., p. 80.
55. Ibid., pp. 241–2.
56. Ibid., p. 246.
57. Ibid., p. 200.
58. Ibid., p. 352.
59. Ibid., p. 39.
60. Ibid., p. 445.
61. Ibid., p. 304.
62. Ibid., p. 314.
63. Ibid., p. 320.

Chapter 3

1. D. H. Lawrence, *Studies in Classic American Literature*, eds. Ezra Greenspan, Lindeth Vasey and John Worthen (Cambridge University Press, 2003), pp. 365–6.
2. Ibid.
3. Ibid.
4. See the chapter entitled 'The Nightmare' in D. H. Lawrence, *Kangaroo*, ed. Bruce Steele (Cambridge University Press, 1994), pp. 212–59.
5. *Women in Love*, p. 481.
6. *The White Peacock*, p. 132.
7. D. H. Lawrence, *The Lost Girl*, ed. John Worthen (Cambridge University Press, 1981), pp. 233–4.
8. *The Lost Girl*, pp. 280–2.
9. At the beginning of the Hardy study, Lawrence complains about the biologists who regard the beauty of poppies as no more than 'the excess which always accompanies reproduction'. See *The 'Study of Thomas Hardy' and Other Essays*, p. 9.
10. Baynes's memoir is reproduced in Mark Kinkead-Weekes, *D. H. Lawrence: From Triumph to Exile*, pp. 602–3.
11. D. H. Lawrence, *The Poems*, ed. Christopher Pollnitz (Cambridge University Press, 2013), vol. 1, pp. 309, 306, 313, 316.
12. *Letters*, eds. Warren Roberts, James T. Boulton and Elizabeth Mansfield (Cambridge University Press, 1987), vol. 4, p. 190.
13. Jessie Chambers, *A Personal Record*, p. 126.

14. D. H. Lawrence, *Mr. Noon*, ed. Lindeth Vasey (Cambridge University Press, 1984), pp. 119–130.
15. Ibid., p. 231.
16. Ibid., p. 209.
17. J. Middleton Murry, *Son of Woman* (London: Jonathan Cape, 1931), pp. 52, 66 and *passim*.
18. *Mr. Noon*, pp. 145–6.
19. Ibid., p. 191.
20. See Ortega y Gasset, *On Love: Aspects of a Single Theme* (New York: Meridian Books, 1957), pp. 19–78 and chapter LIX in *De l'amour*.
21. *The Poems*, vol. 1, p. 517.
22. D. H. Lawrence, *'The Fox', 'The Captain's Doll' and 'The Ladybird'*, ed. Dieter Mehl (Cambridge University Press, 1992), pp. 79, 118, 150–1.
23. The crucial part of the letter is reproduced in Mark Kinkead-Weekes, *From Triumph to Exile*, p. 855.
24. See D. H. Lawrence, *'Twilight in Italy' and Other Essays*, ed. Paul Eggert (Cambridge University Press, 1994), pp. 175–6.
25. *From Triumph to Exile*, p. 704.
26. The introduction can be found in the Cambridge edition of *Introductions and Reviews*. For this remark see p. 18.
27. *'Reflections in the Death of a Porcupine' and Other Essays*, p. 473.
28. *Introductions and Reviews*, p. 64.
29. Ibid., pp. 64–5.
30. D. H. Lawrence, *Aaron's Rod*, ed. Mara Kalnins (Cambridge University Press, 1988), pp. 100, 105.
31. Ibid., pp. 166–7.
32. Walt Whitman, *The Complete Poems,* ed. Francis Murphy (Penguin Books, 1975), p. 301.
33. *Aaron's Rod*, p. 264.
34. Ibid., p. 96.
35. Ibid., p. 89.
36. Ibid., p. 262.
37. Ibid., p. 257.
38. Ibid., p. 262.
39. Ibid., p. 307.

CHAPTER 4

1. *Kangaroo*, pp. 169–176.
2. D. H. Lawrence, *Sea and Sardinia*, ed. Mara Kalnins (Cambridge University Press, 1997), pp. 23–4.
3. *Women in Love*, p. 200.
4. *Kangaroo*, p. 171.

5. Ibid., p. 147.
6. *Women in Love*, p. 206.
7. *Kangaroo*, p. 143.
8. See the chapter in *Women in Love* entitled 'The Industrial Magnate'.
9. *Kangaroo*, p. 114.
10. Ibid., p. 208.
11. Ibid., p. 95.
12. Ibid., p. 107.
13. It is sometimes suggested that 'bi-sexual' and 'bi-sexuality' are terms too crude to apply to a complicated case like Lawrence's. Yet it is difficult to know how else to refer to those who are sexually aroused by the bodies of both their own and the opposite gender.
14. *Women in Love*, p. 107.
15. *Kangaroo*, p. 341.
16. D. H. Lawrence, *The Plumed Serpent*, ed. L. D. Clark (Cambridge University Press, 1990), pp. 367–9.
17. Ibid., pp. 207, 272.
18. See *Letters*, vol. 4, pp. 439, 442, 450.
19. 'The Fox', 'The Captain's Doll' and 'The Ladybird', pp. 157–221. When reading about these figures it is hard not to be reminded of Lawrence's argument with Alan Chambers over Schopenhauer's claim that white skin was not natural to mankind. See p. 13 above.
20. *The Plumed Serpent*, p. 311.
21. Ibid., p. 422.
22. Mark Kinkead-Weekes, *From Triumph to Exile*, p. 551.
23. See R. P. Draper (ed.), *D. H. Lawrence: The Critical Heritage* (London: Routledge and Kegan Paul), p. 344.
24. D. H. Lawrence, '*The Woman Who Rode Away' and Other Stories*, eds. Dieter Mehl and Christa Jansohn (Cambridge University Press, 1995), p. 60.
25. Kate Millet, *Sexual Politics* (London: Hart-Davis, 1971), p. 292.
26. Ibid., p. 286.
27. Ibid.
28. See *Letters*, vol. 6, eds. James T. Boulton and Margaret Boulton, with Gerald M. Lacy (Cambridge University Press, 1991), p. 70.
29. The story can be found in '*The Woman Who Rode Away' and Other Stories*, pp. 211–29.
30. Compare, in *Sons and Lovers*, 'He hated [Miriam] bitterly at that moment, because he made her suffer' (p. 261).
31. Ibid., pp. 82–3 ('He seemed to hate the doll so intensely, because he had broken it').
32. '*The Woman Who Rode Away' and Other Stories*, p. 188.
33. D. H. Lawrence, '*St. Mawr' and Other Stories*, ed. Brian Finney (Cambridge University Press, 1983), pp. 26, 43, 44, 155.
34. '*Reflections on the Death of a Porcupine' and Other Essays*, p. 10.

35. Ibid., p. 332.
36. See '*The Study of Thomas Hardy' and Other Essays*, p. 171.
37. '*Reflections on the Death of a Porcupine' and Other Essays*, p. 336.
38. Ibid., p. 343. For a more extensive treatment of this topic, see my 'Lawrence, Wordsworth and "Anthropomorphic Lust"', *Cambridge Quarterly*, vol. 23, no.3 (1994), pp. 230–42.
39. '*St. Mawr' and Other Stories*, p. 144.
40. '*The Border-Line*' is in '*The Woman Who Rode Away' and Other Stories*. For this extract see p. 96.
41. Ibid., p. 98.

Chapter 5

1. *Letters,* vol. 4, p. 480.
2. See *Late Essays and Articles*, pp. 44, 43, 46–7.
3. Ibid., p. 47.
4. D. H. Lawrence, '*Sketches of Etruscan Places' and Other Essays*, ed. Simonetta de Filippis (Cambridge University Press, 1992), p. 53.
5. See '*England My England' and Other Stories*, ed. Bruce Steele (Cambridge University Press, 1990), pp. 92–107. Although Lawrence wanted to call this story 'Hadrian', it appeared under its original title of 'You Touched Me'.
6. For this essay see D. H. Lawrence, *Mornings in Mexico*, ed. Virginia Crosswhyte Hyde (Cambridge University Press, 2009), pp. 77–94.
7. D. H. Lawrence, '*The Virgin and the Gipsy' and Other Stories*, eds. Michael Herbert, Bethan Jones and Lindeth Vasey (Cambridge University Press, 2005), p. 5 but see pp. 6–7 for the 'snowflower' references and p. 93 above for the way they correlate with a reference in *Mr. Noon*.
8. See 'A Propos of *Lady Chatterley's Lover*' in the Cambridge edition of *Lady Chatterley's Lover*, p. 333.
9. '*The Virgin and the Gipsy' and Other Stories*, p. 78.
10. *Letters*, vol. 4, p. 321.
11. D. H. Lawrence, *The First and Second Lady Chatterley Novels*, eds. Dieter Mehl and Christa Jansohn (Cambridge University Press, 1999), pp. 211–12.
12. These words can be found in the second version of *Lady Chatterley's Love*. See p. 229 in *The First and Second Lady Chatterley Novels*.
13. Ibid., pp. 13, 30, 29.
14. Ibid., p. 55.
15. Ibid., p. 65.
16. See Michel Crouzet, *M. Myself ou La Vie de Stendhal* (Paris: Kimé, 2012), p. 280.
17. *The First and Second Lady Chatterley Novels*, p. 106.
18. Ibid., pp. 39, 68.

19. George Neville, *A Memoir of D. H. Lawrence*, p. 83.

20. *The First and Second Lady Chatterley Novels*, p. 132.

21. Ibid., pp. 113, 112.

22. *The Escaped Cock*, sometimes also known as *The Man Who Died*, can be found in *'The Virgin and the Gipsy' and Other Stories*, pp. 123–63.

23. *Lady Chatterley's Lover*, p. 114.

24. *The First and Second Lady Chatterley Novels*, p. 385.

25. 'A Propos of *Lady Chatterley's Lover*', p. 333.

26. *The First and Second Lady Chatterley Novels*, pp. 41–2; *Lady Chatterley's Lover*, p. 49.

27. *Lady Chatterley's Lover*, p. 39.

28. Ibid., p. 44.

29. See *Lady Chatterley's Lover*, p. 291.

30. *Frieda Lawrence: The Memoirs and Correspondence*, ed. E. W. Tedlock (London: Heinemann, 1961), p. 352.

31. For one account of this episode, see my own *D. H. Lawrence; Dying Game*, pp. 292–5.

32. *The First and Second Lady Chatterley Novels*, p. 101.

33. *The Poems*, vol. 1, p. 440. The poem is called 'Man reaches a point'.

34. *The First and Second Lady Chatterley Novels*, pp. 103, 315, 532.

35. *Women in Love*, p. 249.

36. *Lady Chatterley's Lover*, pp. 209–10.

37. *Sexual Politics*, pp. 239–40.

38. *Lady Chatterley's Lover*, pp. 123, 176.

39. *The Trial of 'Lady Chatterley'*, ed. C. H. Rolph (London: Penguin Books, 1961), p. 70.

40. *Lady Chatterley's Lover*, pp. 246–7.

41. Sparrow's remarks were published in the London journal *Encounter* in February 1962.

42. *Lady Chatterley's Lover*, p. 251.

43. Ibid., pp. 125–6.

44. Ibid., p. 127.

45. For 'Kiss' see *D. H. Lawrence's Paintings*, with an introduction by Keith Sagar (London: Chaucer Press, 2003), p. 58.

46. *Sexual Politics*, p. 241.

47. *Lady Chatterley's Lover*, p. 141.

48. Ibid., p. 71.

49. Ibid., pp. 222–3.

50. *D. H. Lawrence's Paintings*, p. 107. For Lawrence's characterisation of this painting see *Letters*, vol. 6, p. 353.

51. *D. H. Lawrence's Paintings*, p. 81.

52. *Late Essays and Articles*, p. 242.

53. 'A Propos of *Lady Chatterley's Lover*', p. 309.

54. *Lady Chatterley's Lover*, p. 223.
55. *Mr. Noon*, pp. 191–2.
56. *The First and Second Lady Chatterley Novels*, pp. 432–3.
57. See *Letters*, vol. 1, p. 345.
58. *A Personal Record*, pp. 81–3.
59. Emile Zola, *Nana*, translated by George Holden (London: Penguin Books, 1972), p. 223.
60. Charles Baudelaire, 'Mon coeur mis á nu', *Oeuvres Complètes* (Paris: Pléiade, 1961), p. 1272.
61. I dealt with this subject in more detail in 'D. H. Lawrence and the Female Body', *Essays in Criticism*, vol. 46, no. 2 (1996), pp. 136–52.
62. *Mr. Noon*, p. 251.
63. *Letters*, vol. 1, p. 392.
64. *The First and Second Lady Chatterley Novels*, pp. 442; *Lady Chatterley's Lover*, p. 223.
65. *Lady Chatterley's Lover*, p. 200.
66. Ibid., pp. 200–1.
67. Ibid., p. 203.
68. Ibid., pp. 201–2.
69. Ibid., pp. 7–8.
70. *Sexual Politics*, p. 240.
71. *Lady Chatterley's Lover*, pp. 71, 54.

CHAPTER 6

1. 'A Propos of *Lady Chatterley's Lover*', p. 312.
2. Roger Fry, *Cézanne: a study of his development* (Hogarth Press, 1927), p. 52.
3. 'Introduction to These Paintings' can be found in *Late Essays and Articles*, pp. 185–226.
4. 'A Propos of *Lady Chatterley's Lover*', p. 308.
5. Ibid., p. 324.
6. *Letters*, vol. 1, p. 503.
7. 'A Propos of *Lady Chatterley's Lover*', pp. 324–5.
8. Ibid., p. 325.
9. *Letters*, vol. 1, p. 477.
10. J. Middleton Murry, *Son of Woman* (London: Cape, 1931), p. 389.
11. See Michael Black, 'Leavis on Lawrence' in *F. R. Leavis: Essays and Documents*, eds. Ian MacKillop and Richard Storer (Sheffield Academic Press, 1995), p. 193.
12. *The Composite Biography of D. H. Lawrence*, vol. 1, p. 71. It is worth comparing the rather different explanation Paul gives to Miriam of why he should not marry her in *Sons and Lovers*: 'you love me so much, you want to put me in your pocket. And I should die there smothered' (p. 461).

13. See 'Myself Revealed' in *Late Essays and Articles*, p. 179.
14. See 'Part Fourth' of Shelley's *Peter Bell the Third* in, for example, *Shelley's Poetry and Prose*, eds. Donald H, Reiman and Neil Fraistat (London: Norton, 2002), p. 351.

INDEX

Texts by Lawrence are marked with an asterisk

A Propos of 'Lady Chatterley's Lover'
   145, 151, 161, 172, 173–9, 180
Aaron's Rod 98, 102–7, 109, 114,
   116, 117
Aldington, Richard 102
Amores 11, 21
Anal intercourse 52, 53, 54, 58, 72,
   106, 157, 158, 162, 189 n.35
Aphrodite 120
Apocalypse Unsealed, The 74
Aristotle 2
Arlen, Michael 172
As You Like It 29
At the Gates 63
Austen, Jane 137
Aztecs, the 122, 136

Bataille, Georges xiii
Baudelaire, Charles 165–6
Baynes, Rosalind 86–91, 95, 97, 170
Beer, John 185 n.6
Birds, Beasts and Flowers 87, 90, 91
Birrell, Francis 56–8, 64
Blake, William 39
Bloomsbury 8, 56
'Border-Line, The' 130–2
Brett, Dorothy 147–8
'Bride, The' 41
Brontë, Charlotte 23
Brontë, Emily 23
Buddha, the 174
Burrows, Louie 24, 25, 26, 29, 164
Byron, Lord 2

Cannan, Mary 98, 99
Captain's Doll, The 96–7
Carlyle, Thomas 2

Carroll, Lewis xiv
Cézanne, Paul 173–4
Chambers, Alan 2, 6, 8, 13, 80, 192
   n.19
Chambers, Jessie 1–5 (and Schopen-
   hauer), 6, 8, 9, 18, 19–21 (the
   'Test on Miriam'), 22–3 ('Last
   words to Miriam'), 23–4 (as Em-
   ily in *The White Peacock*), 25, 26,
   29, 60–1 (and the 'Prologue' to
   Women in Love), 92, 125, 164,
   167, 179, 180 (and Willie Hop-
   kin), 186 n.9
Chaucer, Geoffrey 173–4
Coleridge, S. T. 2
Collected Poems 11
Cooper, Fennimore 77
Corke, Helen 14, 18, 19, 25, 168
Cowan, James xii
Crown, The 62, 100

Darwin, Charles 4 ('pre-Darwinian')
Daughters of the Vicar 31, 32, 34,
   136, 139, 145
David, (the Biblical King) 114
Dax, Alice 25–6, 29
De Quincey, Thomas 2
Deleuze, Gilles xiii
Dircks, Mrs. Rudolph 2
Dolittle, Hilda ('H. D.') 102
Don Giovanni 95
Dora (her case history) 158
Douglas, Norman 97, 98, 99, 100,
   101, 102, 150
Duncan, Isadora 98

Eliot, George 144

Eliot, T. S. 154–5
Ellis, Havelock 68
*Escaped Cock, The 142, 182
*Etruscan Places, Sketches of 182
Etruscan tombs, tour of 134–5, 136, 139, 142

*Fantasia of the Unconscious 12, 40, 41, 42, 77, 178
Fielding, Henry 94 ('Fieldingesque')
*'Fig' 90
*First Lady Chatterley, The 138–143, 145, 149, 185 n.6
Forster, E. M. 55–6, 58, 121
Foucault, Michel xiii
Freud, Sigmund 1, 18, 24, 34, 36–41 (DHL argues the case against him), 42, 61, 68, 93, 120 (clitoral and vaginal orgasm), 123 (and Millett), 158, 172, 177, 179
'Freudian' xiii, 24, 36, 38, 39, 42, 74, 158, 164, 180–1
'On the Universal Tendency to Debasement in the Sphere of Love' 18, 61, 179
Fry, Roger 173–4

Galsworthy, John xiv (DHL's essay about him)
Ganymede 112
Garnett, David ('Bunny') 43, 56–8, 64, 79, 95, 179
Garnett, Edward 11, 20, 36, 37, 64, 179
Gaskell, Elizabeth 23
Gladstone, Mrs. Catherine 110
*Goats and Compasses 63
Goethe, Johann Wolfgang von 95
Gogh, Vincent van 129
Gogol, Nicolai 2
Grant, Duncan 57–8
Gray, Effie 163
Gross, Otto 34, 36, 37, 40, 42
Guattari, Félix xiii

*'Hadrian' 193 n.5
Hamlet 37
Hardy, Thomas 9 (Jude the Obscure), 12
Harris, Frank 154 (My Life and Loves)
Hawthorne, Nathaniel 77
Hazlitt, William 16 (Libor Amoris)
Heine, Heinrich 2
Heinemann, William 36
Hera 112
Heuffer, Ford Maddox 25, 181
Hobbes, Thomas 39
Hobson, Harold 43, 44, 95
Homosexuality 8, 9, 13, 26, 53, 54, 55–64 (Bloomsbury and Cambridge), 71, 79, 97, 98, 100–1 (in the French Foreign Legion), 158, 159, 168, 169
Hopkin, Willie 180
*'Hopi Snake Dance, The' 136
Huitzilopochtli 117
*'Hymn to Priapus' 40

*'Introduction to These Paintings' 173–4

Jennings, Blanche 6, 13
Jesus 142, 174
*John Thomas and Lady Jane (the 'second version' of Lady Chatterley's Lover) 143, 144, 149, 163–6 (Parkin and pubic hair), 193 n.12
Johnson, Doctor Samuel xv
Jonathan (the Bible's) 7, 44
Joyce, James 150
Jung, Carl xiii ('Jungian'), 39, 42

*Kangaroo 109–16, 117, 128, 140
Keynes, Maynard 56–7, 61, 64, 98
Kouyoumdjian, Dikran (aka Michael Arlen) 172
Krafft-Ebing, Richard von 68

Lady Chatterley's Lover xi-xii (Mellors), xiii, 2, 3, 30, 136, 144, 147, 150–1 (romantic pastoral?), 151–4 (description of Mellors naked and aroused), 154–6 (love), 156–63 (exorcising shame), 166–72 (Mellors's sexual history), 173, 182, 185 n.6
  the trial xiv, 156, 170
Ladybird, The 119
Last Tango in Paris 157
*'Last Words to Miriam' 21, 91, 158
*'Last Words to Muriel' 21
Lawrence, Ernest 1
Lawrence, Frieda 15, 21, 26, 29 (first meeting), 30, 31, 33 (DHL's expressions of love), 34–6 (attitude to DHL and philosophy of life), 37 (talked about Oedipus), 38, 39, 41–2 (her disgust at DHL's poems about his mother), 43, 44, 46, 47, 48, 49, 53 (taking her as a dog does a bitch), 54, 58, 59 (prevented from seeing her children), 66 (Frieda and comfort sex), 80, 81, 86, 87, 89, 92–4 (in *Mr. Noon*), 95 (denies Murry's claims about Lawrence's failure to satisfy her), 97, 98, 106 (and extra-marital affairs), 110–1 (as the 'qb'), 114, 116 (given ranch by Mabel Sterne), 119, 121, 126 (goes to Europe alone), 127, 129, 130–2 (portrayed in 'The Border-Line'), 133, 136, 147 (her remarks on *Lady Chatterley's Lover*), 148, 149, 150 (unfaithful but constant?), 151, 165, 170 (and Bertha Coutts), 179, 180–2 (the best thing that ever happened to DHL?), 189 n. 35
Lawrence, Mrs. Gertrude 1, 24, 28, 40

as 'his mother' 1, 24, 29, 37, 38, 40, 41–2 (DHL's poems after her death), 43, 92, 94, 133, 188 n.21
Leavis, F. R. xii, xv, 11, 166, 180
Lodge, David 92
Look! We Have Come Through! 15, 46, 47, 50, 92, 94
Lost Girl, The 81–6, 87, 91, 98, 119
*'Love among the Haystacks' 13, 31, 34
*'Love Was Once a Little Boy' 128–30
*'Love' 128
Low, Ivy 37, 38
Luhan, Mabel 122, 124, 127, 132 (for other references see 'Sterne, Mabel')
Luhan, Tony 119

Mackenzie, Compton 38, 121
Magnus, Maurice xv, 97–101, 102
*'Making Love to Music' 134
*'Man reaches a point' 149
Mann, Thomas 11 (*Death in Venice*)
Mansfield, Katherine 130
Marcus Aurelius 2
Maupassant, Guy de 66
Mazzini, Giuseppe 2
Melville, Herman 77
Memoirs of the Foreign Legion by M.M. (Maurice Magnus) 173–4
Middleton, Richard 54
Mill on the Floss, The 137
Millett, Kate 121–6, 153, 154, 157, 158, 171
Mohammed 138
Montaigne, Michel de 2
Moore, George xi
*'Morality and the Novel' 129
Mornings in Mexico 182
Morrell, Lady Ottoline 56, 60, 61
Murry, John Middleton 53, 62, 94, 130–2 (in 'The Border-Line'), 133, 148, 180, 189 n.35

Mussolini, Benito 138
*'My Love, My Mother' 42

*Mr. Noon 92–5, 105, 149, 162, 165, 193 n.7
Narcissus 13
Neville, George xi, 7, 8, 19, 25, 92, 141, 163–5, 166
*'New Eve and Old Adam' 43–6, 47, 48, 69, 106
*'New Heaven and Earth' 15
Nietzschean 86, 145
*'None of That!' 124, 125, 127
Nouvelle Helöise, La 3

Oedipus 1 ('oedipal phase'), 37, 38 ('oedipal'), 39
Orestes 114
Ortega y Gasset 95
Osiris 142

Pan 119
*Paul Morel 37
Persepolis 167
Plato 2, 57, 174
*Plumed Serpent, The 116–121, 122, 138, 170, 182
Poe, Edgar Alan 77
Pope, the 175
Pound, Ezra 25
*'Prologue' to Women in Love 58–63
Proust 26 ('Proustian'), 150
*'Prussian Officer, The' 124, 125–6
Pryce, James 74, 81
Psychoanalytical Review, The 38
Pylades 114

*Quetzlcoatl 116, 117, 119, 122

*Rainbow, The 16–17, 30 (coup de foudre), 48, 49–52 (Will and Anna's sex life), 53, 59, 64–5 (Ursula and Skrebensky), 66, 67, 68, 69, 71

(Ursula and her schoolmistress), 82, 93, 107, 160, 169
Rape of the Sabine Women (DHL's painting of) 159
Ravagli, Angelo 148–9
*'Reality of Peace, The' 62–3
*Reflections on the Death of a Porcupine 128
Richthoven, Manfred von 59
Richthovens, the 34
Romeo and Juliet 3, 29, 31
Rubens, Peter Paul 159 ('Rubenesque')
Ruskin, John 163, 179
Russell, Betrand 55, 56–7
Russell, Ken 90

Saint Paul 25, 142 ('Pauline')
Savage, Henry 54, 55, 80
Schiller, Friedrich 2
Schopenhauer, Arthur 1–5 'Metaphysics of Love'), 27, 31, 32, 33, 38, 39, 85, 86, 88, 178, 192 n.19
Schopenhaurean 31, 90
*Sea and Sardinia 110–11
Seneca 2
*'Shades of Spring' 187 n.21
Shakespeare, William 173–4
Shallot, Lady of 137, 173
Shaw, George Bernard 175
*'She said as well to me' 47
Shelley, Percy Bysshe 2, 181
Sheridan, Thomas 2
Signature, The 62
*Sisters, The 48, 59
Son of Woman (Murry's) 94, 95
*Sons and Lovers xi, 1, 9, 10, 19, 21–2 (treatment of Miriam), 24, 25, 26, 36–8 ('Freudian' influences on final version), 42, 48, 89, 124–5 (sacrifice of Arabella), 167, 179 (representative?), 182, 186 n.6, 187 n.29, 195 n.11
Sorrows of Young Werther, The 3, 95

Sparrow, John 156, 157
Spilka, Mark xii
*'Spirits Summoned West' 188 n.21
*St. Mawr 126
stellar polarity (Birkin's conception of) 71, 79, 102, 103, 118
Stendhal 9, 11, 16, 17, 31, 95 ('Stendhalian'), 141
    De l'amour 31, 141, 149
    Le rouge et le noir 11, 35
Sterne, Mabel 116, 119 (for other references see 'Luhan, Mabel')
Strachey, Lytton 56
Stracheys, the 57
*Studies in Classic American Literature 77
*'Study of Thomas Hardy' 9, 88, 190 n.9
Swift, Jonathan 2, 161

Taylor, Rachel Annand 188 n.21
Tietjens, Eunice 63
Timbuctoo 167
*Tortoise poems, the 90, 91
*'Tortoise Shout' 90–1
*Trespasser, The 11, 14, 19, 81
Turner, Reggie 97
*Twilight in Italy 99

*Virgin and the Gypsy, The 133, 136–8, 139, 173
*'Virgin Mother, The' 41
*'Virgin Youth' 10–11, 13
Walker, Sarah 16
Weekley, Barbara ('Barby') 133, 134, 136, 138, 140, 146
Weekley children, the 133

Weekley, Elsa 126
Weekley, Ernest 29, 33, 34, 43, 59, 136, 162, 166
*'Weeknight Service' 15
*White Peacock, The 6–7 (bathing scene), 8, 19, 22–3 (Emily), 38, 54, 61, 80 (Annabel), 104, 114
Whitman, Walt 77–81, 102–3 ('Dalliance of Eagles'), 104, 113, 155
*'Wild Common, The' 13
Wilde, Oscar 57, 96 ('Wildean')
Wittgenstein, Ludwig xii
*'Woman Who Rode Away, The' 122–125, 143
*Women in Love i, xi, 30, 48, 53, 59, 60 (upset Lady Ottoline), 61 (naked wrestling), 64, 66–7 (Gerald's night-time visit to Gudrun), 67–9 (sado-masochism?), 70–5 (Birkin and love), 77, 82, 88, 90 (Ken Russell film), 97, 103, 104, 105–6, 111, 112 (Blutbrüdershaft), 113, 114, 115 (Birkin rolls in the wet vegetation), 151
Woolf, Virginia 150
Wordsworth, William 14, 15, 116 ('Wordsworthian'), 129–30 (Peter Bell), 181
Wuthering Heights 23

*'You Touched Me' 193 n.5

Zola, Emile 164

ACKNOWLEDGEMENTS

This book is closely associated with a talk I gave at the international conference on D. H. Lawrence which was held in Gargnano, Italy, in June 2014. I would like to thank the officers of the D. H. Lawrence Society of North America for inviting me to that event, and particularly its then president, Betsy Wallace. Sally Minogue, of Christ Church University in Canterbury, gave me much useful advice on a first draft, as did my former student (who is now at the University of Manchester), Howard Booth; and in its final stages Neil Roberts has been very helpful. My chief debt is indicated by my dedication. Through many years of warm friendship and (on occasions) equally warm discussion, I have admired the way John Worthen has been able to publish important work on the English Romantics, Robert Schumann and T. S. Eliot whilst at the same time establishing himself as the world's leading authority on all matters Lawrentian.

For permission to quote from an essay on Whitman, which only saw the light of day quite recently, I would like to thank Pollinger Ltd., the firm established eighty years ago by the man who had been Lawrence's own literary agent.

Lightning Source UK Ltd.
Milton Keynes UK
UKHW041622220620
365391UK00009B/2482